What You Need to Know About Kabbalah

THE TEACHINGS OF KABBALAH SERIES

What You Need to Know About Kabbalah

Rabbi Yitzchak Ginsburgh

Edited by Rabbi Moshe Genuth

Gal Einai

Jerusalem

THE TEACHINGS OF KABBALAH SERIES

WHAT YOU NEED TO KNOW ABOUT KABBALAH

Rabbi Yitzchak Ginsburgh

Edited by Rabbi Moshe Genuth

Printed in the United States of America and Israel
First Edition

For information:

USA: Dwelling Place Publishing
      11025 Larkwood, Suite #1423
      Houston, TX 77096
      Tel.: (866) 393-5575

Israel: GAL EINAI
      PO Box 1015
      Kfar Chabad 72915
      tel.: +972-3-9608008

E-mail: ge@inner.org

Web: www.inner.org

      GAL EINAI produces and publishes books, pamphlets,
      and recorded lectures by Rabbi Yitzchak Ginsburgh. To
      receive a catalog of our products in English and/or
      Hebrew, please contact us at any of the above addresses,
      email ge@inner.org, or visit our website.

Text Layout: David Hillel
Cover Design: Shmuel Kaffe

ISBN: 965-7146-119

Table of Contents

INTRODUCTION

Introduction

The Hebrew word Kabbalah has become the standard term used for referring to the vast array of mystical thought and practice revealed and handed down as part of the Jewish tradition. The popular use of this term dates back to the late 12th century. Before then, Judaism's mystical teachings were known by other names.[1]

Kabbalah is usually translated as "received tradition."[2] In this sense, Kabbalah conveys the continuity of a tradition that has been passed down from generation to generation. But, originally, in the Torah,[3] Kabbalah comes from the verb meaning "to correspond." One might ask: What does correspondence have to do with mysticism?

The short answer is that everything that we know about the world we know by corresponding one thing to another. We draw parallels or correspondences between those things that we are familiar with and those that we are not. This is especially true when the subjects of our inquiry are the hidden, secret, and concealed aspects of reality. To understand that which is driving and guiding our reality, we must first understand the basic mystical models and then learn to correctly apply them to any given situation in life.

The basis for drawing such correspondences is the essential unity of creation and the single Divine root from which everything emanates. Were the Creator not a singular Unity, the essence of Oneness itself, we might not be justified in doing so and might come to misunderstandings about the hidden dimensions of our reality.[4] The Kabbalistic methodology (both theoretical and practical) is based on the construction of correspondences between the revealed and concealed aspects of reality.[5] By correctly analyzing our subject of interest based on traditional Kabbalistic models, we are able to understand its past, present, and future; we are able to tap into the process of creation that brought it about, to navigate its present reality with meaning and direction, and to recognize the future possibilities that it holds.

The ability to take Divinely revealed models given to us by the prophets and to correspond them correctly depends on the development of our super-rational sensitivity to God's inherent and absolute Unity. Thus, Kabbalah should be taught in a way that nurtures our capacity to be sensitive to the Divine in reality.

Kabbalah, in the sense of "received wisdom," refers to the teachings passed down from generation to generation aimed at increasing our sensibility to God's Unity. Thus, Kabbalah focuses on God and His relationship with us. It reveals the deepest secrets about the Creator's nature, creative power, primordial plan for creation, the manner in which His supernal realm functions, and the ways of His Providence on earth.

Whereas in earlier generations the study of Kabbalah was reserved for the select few, the holy Rabbi Isaac Luria, the Arizal, whose definitive teachings dominate Kabbalah to this day states that in the generations before the coming of the Messiah, it is permissible and even an obligation to reveal to the world the hidden wisdom of the Torah. Rabbi Israel Ba'al Shem Tov, the founder of Chassidut, writes as well that the dissemination of these mysteries "to the furthest extremes" will enable the Mashiach to come and the ultimate vision of a rectified world to become a reality.[6]

The Revelation of Kabbalah

Kabbalah is the inner dimension of the Torah in its widest sense, i.e., both the Written Torah (the Bible) and the Oral Tradition. Therefore, it is impossible to see Kabbalah as anything but the deepest explanation of the secrets of the Torah.

More specifically, Kabbalah is a composite of prophecy and wisdom.[7] Historically, Kabbalah developed out of the prophetic spirit that existed in Judaism for over a millennium and a half; beginning with Abraham (20th century BCE) and stretching all the way to the second Temple period (4th century BCE). Unfortunately, the nature of prophecy is commonly vulgarized. Though prophecy includes visions of the future, its main purpose has always been to see the Divine. It is through prophecy that God reveals Himself and His will to human beings.[8]

The spirit of prophecy that had filled individual prophets continued to hover over and inspire the Jewish people as a community even after the destruction of the first Temple. But, this spirit could no longer manifest directly. Instead, the appreciation of the Divine was manifest by the wisdom of the Oral Torah (the Oral Tradition), the body of Rabbinic knowledge that began developing in the second Temple period and continues to this day. One of the central differences between wisdom and prophecy is that wisdom is given to one who has studied and developed his or her rational mind ("wisdom is given to the wise"[9]) and if one invests sufficient effort in the search for truth, one will certainly be rewarded with finding even more than could initially be imagined.[10] The spirit of prophecy, on the other hand, cannot so surely be aroused from below, whether by wisdom or by righteousness (though these are certainly necessary prerequisites for attaining prophecy); it is entirely a God-send, and as such is essentially super-rational.

Thus, the essence of Kabbalah can be described as the union of the rational mind (the wisdom of the Oral Torah) with the super-rational (the prophetic spirit, which remains to this day).

From the time of its revelation at Mt. Sinai, the concealed dimension of the Torah—that is, Kabbalah—was known only to priests and prophets. However, after prophecy ceased and the Temple in Jerusalem was destroyed, a new era began. In approximately 100 CE, Rabbi Shimon Bar Yochai—also known by his acronym, Rashbi—was given the power and permission from Heaven to reveal to his disciples the inner wisdom of Kabbalah.

He introduced and explained the most basic Kabbalistic model, that of the ten *sefirot*. The *sefirot* are emanations of Divine light, or energy, which lie at the heart of anything and everything in our universe. Rashbi revealed the function of each *sefirah* (the singular form of *sefirot*) by showing how the *sefirot* manifest themselves in every verse of the Torah and every phenomenon of nature. His teachings are contained in the great classic text of Kabbalah, *Sefer HaZohar* (The Book of Splendor), known simply as the *Zohar*.

For some one thousand years after the passing of Rabbi Shimon Bar Yochai, the teachings of the *Zohar* were privately transmitted from one Kabbalist to another. In each generation only a few select scholars of the Torah were deemed worthy of preserving the *Zohar's* teachings.

In was not until the 13th century that the *Zohar* was disseminated publicly. At that time, in Spain, Rabbi Moshe de Leon (1240-1305), a Kabbalist who had been given a copy of the *Zohar* from earlier generations, decided to make it public. However, only a very few could comprehend its teachings. For the next 250 years, many Kabbalists attempted to provide a conceptual framework within which to place the loosely associated and highly symbolic lessons of the *Zohar*.

None was as successful as the great Talmudic scholar and Kabbalist, Rabbi Moshe Cordevero of Safed (1522-1570), better known as the Ramak. The Ramak's goal was to rationally systematize all of Kabbalistic thought up to his time, in particular the teachings of the *Zohar*.

In his magnum opus, *Pardes Rimonim* (The Pomegranate Orchard), the Ramak demonstrated the underlying unity of Kabbalistic tradition by organizing the various, often seemingly contradictory, teachings of the hidden wisdom into a coherent system.

The core of the Ramak's system consists of a detailed description of how God, through the means of the ten *sefirot*, **evolved** finite reality out of the exclusive expanse of infinite Divine Light referred to as *Or Ein Sof* (infinite light).

Almost immediately upon the Ramak's demise, Rabbi Isaac Luria (1534-1572), popularly referred to as the holy Ari, or the Arizal, commenced the next stage in the revelation of Kabbalah. The Ari was born in Jerusalem but subsequently relocated to Egypt where he was quickly recognized as a Talmudic prodigy. Introduced to the secrets of the Kabbalah by one of his mentors, he would often spend extended periods in isolated meditation. During one of his visionary experiences, the Ari was instructed by the prophet Elijah to return to the Land of Israel, where, in the city of Safed, he would find the one destined to become his chief disciple and exponent of his teachings.

According to tradition, the Ari arrived in Safed on the very day of the Ramak's funeral. Joining the procession, he envisioned a pillar of fire over the Ramak's bier—a sign that one is meant to inherit the deceased's mantle of leadership.

The Ari patiently waited for half a year, making no direct overture, until such time as his destined disciple, Rabbi Chayim Vital (1543-1620), presented himself for instruction. The Ari only lived for another two years (he died at the age of 38), but in that short period he managed to reveal a completely new path and depth in the study of the *Zohar* in particular and in the inner dimension of all parts of the Torah, in general. So pivotal were his insights that to this day the study of Kabbalah is virtually synonymous with the study of the Ari's writings.

At the center of the Ari's system is a radically new description of the evolution of reality. Unlike the Ramak, who saw the forces of creation as seemingly autonomous from one another and linearly advancing in an evolutionary manner, the Ari saw a constellation of forces in active dialogue with one another at every stage of that evolution. He described the *sefirot* not as zero-dimensional points, or even one-dimensional lines or strings, but as complex and dynamically interacting entities known as *partzufim* (personae) each with a symbolically human-like character.

According to the Ari, the creative forces exist as the concealed inner dimension of reality (**enclothed** within it) and thus continue to interact with it continually responding to the way human beings manage the perennial conflict between good and evil. In this way, the impact of human actions on the *sefirot*—which channel Divine energy into the world—can either facilitate or impede the progress of creation toward its planned final state of perfection.

Subsequent to the Ari, there was one more personality who inspired a qualitative shift in the evolution of Kabbalistic thought. This was Rabbi Yisrael Ba'al Shem Tov (1698-1760). Born in the Podolian province of western Ukraine, the Ba'al Shem Tov devoted the early part of his life to helping ease the physical and spiritual distress of his fellow Jews while at the same time delving into the mysteries of Kabbalah with a fraternity of mystics known as the *Nistarim* (the concealed ones). In 1734 he revealed himself as a Kabbalist and healer and proceeded to found a popular movement that was to reinvigorate the spiritual lives of Jews all across Eastern Europe. This movement, which came to be known as Chassidut (or, Hassidism, as it is sometimes spelled in English) was inwardly based upon the ancient doctrinal tradition of Kabbalah, while outwardly giving new emphasis to the simple and joyful service of God, particularly through prayer and acts of loving-kindness.[11]

It was the Ba'al Shem Tov's disciples, particularly Rabbi Shneur Zalman of Liadi (1745-1812), the author of the *Tanya* and the founder of the Chabad branch of Chassidut, who brought to light the Ba'al Shem Tov's profound understanding of Kabbalistic thought. In Chassidic thought, the abstract and often impenetrable formulae of classic Kabbalah are recast into the descriptive language and experiences of the human psyche and soul. By using our inner experience of personhood as an allegorical model for understanding the deepest mysteries of the universe, Chassidut was able to both elevate the consciousness of the ordinary Jew as well as expand the conceptual territory of Kabbalistic thought.

It is a common misconception that Chassidut is a movement existing outside the formal mainstream of Kabbalah. In fact, not only did the Ba'al Shem Tov influence Kabbalistic thought, he brought it to its historical apex, both in terms of its conceptual refinement and its degree of influence upon the lives of the Jewish populace. While Kabbalistic knowledge until the Ba'al Shem Tov is described as the "soul of the Torah,"[12] Chassidut is called "the soul within the soul."[13]

Three Systems of Kabbalah

In Chassidic thought it has been pointed out[14] that from a wider perspective the development of Kabbalah followed a path that highlights the three different conceptual schemes found in its wisdom. These three schemes are known as: *evolution* (הִשְׁתַּלְשְׁלוּת), *enclothement* (הִתְלַבְּשׁוּת), and *omnipresence* (הַשְׁרָאָה). Each formed the conceptual and systemic core of the teachings taught by the Ramak, the Arizal, and the Ba'al Shem Tov, respectively.

In the *evolutionary* scheme (not to be confused with the scientific theory of the same name) the complexity of our own reality is described as unfolding by a process of cause and effect out of the Absolute Oneness of the Creator. At any point in time, the universe's state can be compared to a chain made of many links, the first of which is the Creator Himself. Though the Ramak was a mystic who derived his main inspiration from the poetic imagery of the *Zohar*, his conceptual use of an evolutionary paradigm allowed him to present the central themes of Kabbalah in a semi-philosophical language. The particular dialect of philosophical discourse was deemed by him as the most effective for describing a process which itself possessed a certain sequential logic and coherence.

The Arizal shifted the operational paradigm of Kabbalah from that of evolutionary development to that of instantaneous interactions, referred to as *enclothement*. Enclothement views every stratum of reality as designed to enclothe itself within another, following the example of how the soul exactly fits within the body. The inner core does not merely precede the outer layer in importance; it also endows it with the life-force and energy it needs to sustain its being. Hence, enclothement is similar to a biological picture of reality, focusing on life-force and its energetic transformations as they dictate the form of the universe.

Reincarnation, one of the Arizal's central topics of interest that we will discuss later, is an example of an enclothement-driven Kabbalistic theme. Though well recognized, it did not find a central place in the Ramak's Kabbalah and, as will shortly be explained, is viewed as relatively restrictive in the context of the Ba'al Shem Tov's Kabbalah.

Finally, the third and most advanced Kabbalistic paradigm introduced by the Ba'al Shem Tov is founded upon the Chassidic stress of the immanent *omnipresence* of the Almighty, which implies a unique equivalence between God and Creation, as expressed in the Chassidic idiom: "God is all and all is God." The proper understanding of this idea, especially in terms of how it differs from the tenets of pantheism, constitutes the supreme Kabbalistic insight of our pre-Messianic age. Although both the system of the Ramak and the Ari play a crucial role in advancing our understanding of God's relationship with creation, they are only rungs on the ladder of consciousness, as we seek full liberation from our own shortcoming and the ability to see God everywhere, even in ourselves, ultimately restoring His absolute and exclusive hold upon reality.

Technically, the Hebrew term used to describe the Ba'al Shem Tov's paradigm is difficult to translate. Its Hebrew root[15] implies the pervasive infiltration of some higher force throughout a lower plane of reality. It is commonly used in reference to the *Shechinah*—God's immanent Presence within the created realm. In the vernacular, it denotes inspiration, implying the encompassing of one's reality by some greater energy which elevates one to an existential plane otherwise unattainable. With omnipresence as the Kabbalistic paradigm, the notion of overlapping realities common to the Arizal gives way to a profounder awareness of God interpenetrating all of reality in equal measure. As we gradually adopt the Ba'al Shem Tov's paradigm and increase the awareness of our identification with God's aggregate Being, our interest in our own past reincarnations lessens and our concern with regard to the fate of our souls is collectivized. Thus, our spiritual energy turns to focus on the fate of our communities, our nation, our land, and ultimately the universe as a whole.

Spreading the Wellsprings of Kabbalah

The Arizal explained that as we approach the Messianic era it becomes critical that the study of Kabbalah be spread. In his words: "it is a *mitzvah* [a commandment] to reveal this wisdom now."[16] This is based on the statement of the *Zohar* that "with this book [i.e., the *Zohar*], they will exit their exile with mercy."[17] The study of the inner dimension of the Torah, as revealed in the *Zohar*, has the power to prevent the difficult traumatic events otherwise required for us to make the transition from our present state of consciousness to the consciousness of the Messianic era. Nonetheless, the Arizal still imposed certain conditions upon those who desired to study Kabbalah.[18]

The Ba'al Shem Tov's advocated a radically new approach. From a spiritual encounter with the Messiah's soul, the Ba'al Shem Tov learnt that the redemption would occur once his (the Ba'al Shem Tov's) wellsprings of teaching would spread forth to the remotest extremes.[19] Subsequently, the Ba'al Shem Tov explained that the remotest extremes specifically refers to those Jews who until now could not have been considered sanctified enough to study Kabbalah. Obviously, spreading the wellsprings of Kabbalah to these extremes means specifically addressing every single Jew, regardless of level of observance or commitment to the Torah. Not only that, but even non-Jews, who also require the wisdom of Kabbalah in order to participate in the redemption in a compassionate and merciful manner, should also be addressed and taught those parts of the wisdom that pertain to them.[20] Because all souls require the wisdom of Kabbalah to uncover their potential and serve their purpose in the world, generally, there are no longer any restricting conditions placed on who may study Kabbalah.

Chassidut is (for now) the final stage in the revelation of Kabbalah. Its interpretative paradigm allows us to understand and internalize the teachings of the *Zohar* and the Arizal as never before. Where the Kabbalah of the Ramak and the Arizal were theoretically inclined,

Chassidut brings the student of Kabbalah to experience the Divine directly. Chassidut reveals the innermost essence of the Divine in such a way that it can be experienced by even those who are furthest from the Almighty. Therefore, Chassidut brings Kabbalah to every single person, Jew, or non-Jew, male and female, young and old alike.

For these reasons, the present volume on Kabbalah is written from the perspective of Chassidut. This is first apparent in the book's structure. One of the most basic models used in the Ba'al Shem Tov's Kabbalah is that of Worlds, Souls, and Divinity (which parallels the Ari's three-part model of vessels, sparks, and lights). This book is therefore divided into three parts, reflecting this three-fold model.

Part I is meant to serve as an introduction to the world of Kabbalah. Torah in general and Kabbalah in particular constitute a world of tradition, associations, and wisdom. Whenever entering into a world the first thing to do is to orient oneself. We have provided a primer in this introduction, but to truly begin to feel comfortable and find one's way around it is necessary to know not just what is in the world of Kabbalah, but also where its borders run. Thus, Part I focuses on the question of what is Kabbalah and just as importantly, what is it not.

Part II deals with the souls of Kabbalah which are the *sefirot* and their experiential equivalents. This part will explain in greater detail how Kabbalistic models are formulated and applied and how their study serves to transform our understanding of ourselves and our surroundings.

Part III is devoted to the Divine. In it we will apply much of what we have learnt already to analyze the Names of God on four different levels. God's Names and connotations form the central core of all Kabbalistic meditation. The final chapter will reveal how it is possible to see the Divine and establish a mature relationship with the Creator at every moment of life.

Acknolwedgments

We would first of all like to thank Yechzekel Anis who wrote the first draft of the present volume. Yechezkel has been a longtime and devoted student of Rabbi Ginsburgh's. We would also like to thank Rabbi Moshe Wisnefsky, Rabbi and Mrs. Asher and Sarah Esther Crispe, and Mrs. Uriellah Obst for their editorial work in the earlier stages.

Notes:

1. For example, in the Talmud, we find *Sitrei Torah*, "Mysteries of the Torah" (*Chagigah* 13a; *Pesachim* 119a); *Ta'amei Torah*, "Reasons of the Torah" (Ibid.); *Ma'aseh Breishit*, "Workings of Creation" (*Chagigah* 11b); and, *Ma'aseh Merkavah*, "Workings of the Chariot" (*Berachot* 21b; *Shabbat* 80b; *Sukah* 28a; *Chagigah* ibid. and elsewhere). For more on these four parts of the esoteric tradition of the Torah see Rabbi Yosef Ergas (1685-1730), *Shomer Emunim (Hakadmon)*.

   In post-Talmudic sources, we find the esoteric tradition referred to as: the Inner Wisdom (*chochmah penimit*), the Wisdom of Truth (*chochmat ha'emet*), the Hidden Wisdom (*chochmah nistarah*), and the Secret (*sod*). See for example Rabbi Meir Ibn Gabbai (1480-c.1540), *Avodat Hakodesh*, part 2, chapter 13.

2. Apparently the first to use the word "Kabbalah" to refer to the Torah's esoteric tradition is Rabbi Elazar of Worms (better known as the *Rokei'ach*, c.1165-c.1230). Before then, in the Talmudic literature, "Kabbalah" referred to both the extra-Pentateuchal parts of the Bible (i.e., the Prophets and the Writings) and to the oral-tradition of the Torah (i.e., the *Midrashim* and the *Mishnah*).

3. Exodus 26:5, 36:12.

4. Incidentally, science uses a similar argument to justify its belief (and this is a belief, there is no proof that this is a true statement) that the physical laws governing the physical aspects of our universe are the same everywhere, i.e., that the entire universe emanated from a single source. The scientific notion of parsimony (as this belief is called) thus depends on God's essential Oneness. Still, science has not come to terms yet with the notion of free-will and how by exercising it to create a relationship with the Creator, human beings have the power to influence and even change the very laws that govern reality.

5. As will be discussed in chapter 4, the basic unit of every Kabbalistic correspondence is a model or template, called a *partzuf*, in Hebrew.

6. In a letter to his brother-in-law, Rabbi Gershon Kitover, *Keter Shem Tov*, 1. See also introduction to *The Hebrew Letters*.

7. For more on the joining of wisdom and prophecy, see p. 34.

8. As in the verse: "I will speak to the prophets and I have afforded many visions and by the hand of the prophet My likeness is revealed" (Hosea 12:11).

9. Daniel 2:21.

10. The sages say that: "[One who says:] 'I have toiled and I have not found'—do not believe. 'I have not toiled and I have found'—do not believe. I have toiled and I have found'—believe!" (*Megilah* 6b).

11. As the *Mishnah* states: "The world endures because of three things: [the study of] the Torah, the worship of God [i.e., prayer], and acts of loving-kindness" (*Avot* 1:2).

12. *Nishmeta De'orayta* (cf. *Zohar* III, 152a).

13. *Nishmeta le'nishmeta*.

14. Rabbi Yitzchak Isaac of Homil (c.1770 to 1857), *Ma'amar Hashiflut Vehasimchah* (A Treatise on Humility and Joy). Rabbi Isaac of Homil, one of the greatest scholars of his day, was the chief Rabbi of his Ukrainian hometown, Homil. A devoted student and disciple of the first three leaders of Chabad, he was a prolific writer who left behind some of the deepest writings in Jewish mysticism.

15. Which is: שׂרה.

16. *Tanya, Igeret Hakodesh* 26.

17. *Zohar* III, 124b.

18. On the part of the teacher it is indeed a *mitzvah* to reveal the hidden teachings, but only to those who are already worthy of integrating them into their lives. The description of what is required of an appropriate student is even outlined in the introduction that appears at the beginning of the classic text of the Arizal's Kabbalah, *Eitz Chaim* (The Tree of Life).

19. In a letter to his brother-in-law, Rabbi Gershon Kitover, *Keter Shem Tov*, 1. See also introduction to *The Hebrew Letters*.

20. Particularly those teachings that focus on the process of creation and Divine Providence over all. See *Kabbalah and Meditation for the Nations*.

PART I

OVERVIEW

...I asked the Mashiach: 'When will the Master come?' And he answered: 'By this you shall know: When your teachings become public and revealed in the world, and your wellsprings burst forth to the farthest extremes... then all the impurities will cease to exist and there will be a time of good will and salvation.'

...this I may inform you and may God help you; your way shall ever be in the Presence of God and never leave your consciousness in the time of your prayer and study: In every word that issues from your lips, intend to unify. For in every letter there are worlds, souls, and Divinity, and they ascend and connect and unify with each other, and afterward the letters connect and unify to become a word, and then unify in true unification in Divinity.... Surely God will be your aid and wherever you turn you will succeed and reach greater awareness.

From a letter by Rabbi Israel Ba'al Shem Tov

What is Kabbalah? 1

KABBALAH IS THE MYSTICAL TRADITION OF THE JEWISH PEOPLE. Although it has gone through many stages of revelation since that time, the beginnings of Kabbalah are to be found almost four thousand years ago, with our first patriarch, Abraham.[1]

The accumulated insights of Kabbalah provide access to the inner dimension of reality and thereby to the experience of God in this world.

Simply put, Kabbalah is the study of God. The students of Kabbalah desire to know God in order to emulate Him[2] and thus to be like Him.

To come close to God, the Creator of the universe, students of Kabbalah seek to intellectually comprehend what might be termed the "physics of creation." The focus of Kabbalah is never the acquisition of wisdom in and of itself; wisdom is only a tool, a bridge to connect us to our Creator through comprehension of the creative process, which is ongoing, dynamic, and constantly responsive to feedback from creation.[3]

Ancient Revelation

The first person who devoted his life to discover and come close to God was Abraham. Due to his great self-sacrifice, many deep secrets of creation were revealed to him, allowing him to experience what he desired most—a closeness and sense of oneness with his Creator. The very first classic text of Kabbalah, *Sefer Yetzirah* (The Book of Formation) is attributed to Abraham.

This basic text of Kabbalah introduces the concept of thirty-two paths of wisdom with which God, and subsequently man, engages in the creative process.[4] The thirty-two paths of wisdom are comprised of:

◆ The ten *sefirot*—the ten emanations of Divine light, which energize the creative process and define its paramaters

◆ The twenty-two letters of the Hebrew alphabet—the building blocks of creation and the channels through which Divine consciousness flows into creation

Abraham passed this wisdom on to his son, Isaac, who passed it on to his son, Jacob, who transmitted it to his twelve sons, the progenitors of the Twelve Tribes of Israel. Seven generations after Abraham, the Children of Israel merited receiving the Torah from God at Mt. Sinai. The Torah contains not only instructions for living a life according to God's will, but also, concealed within it, the blueprint the the Almighty used to create the universe and everything in it.

Thus, the Torah has two aspects to it: the revealed and the concealed, which are also referred to as its body and its soul[5]:

◆ The body of the Torah (*gufei Torah*[6]) comprises the laws that govern our daily behavior. These laws express the will of God for our ultimate and absolute good in this world and the World to Come. This aspect of the Torah is also called the Torah's revealed dimension (*nigleh*).

◆ The soul of the Torah (*nishmeta de'orayta*), i.e., Kabbalah, comprises the secrets relating to God as the Creator, the process of creation, and God's Providence over creation. These secrets possess many dimensions of mysteries and mysteries within mysteries. This aspect of the Torah is also referred to as its concealed dimension (*nistar*).[7]

God gives us the understanding of both dimensions of the Torah because He desires that we become partners with Him in the process of creation[8] and that we be worthy to receive the ultimate reward of becoming one with Him. We do so when we freely choose to align our will with His will. To do so entails a commitment to living by the commandments of the Torah, delving into its mysteries, and devoting our lives, like Abraham, to bring into the world's consciousness transcendent and infinite light, light that appeared at the outset of creation but that subsequently became hidden from human eyes.[9]

The Appeal of Kabbalah

All souls intuit the existence of a deeper reality than that which can be perceived with the body's five senses. The Jewish soul, especially, is imbued with the desire and need to be in contact with the invisible, hidden dimension of reality.

Very often, the material world and the initial impression that Jews sometimes receive with regard to their religion convey the mistaken idea that it is impossible to reach the hidden dimension of reality. And as a result, some people just give up, numbed by the banality of physical existence.

However, our age is witness to many seekers who are not so easily diverted from this most fundamental need of the soul—to seek the inner meaning of life and reality, to seek God Himself.

When such individuals hear for the first time that Judaism possesses an inner secret teaching called Kabbalah, they are immediately attracted. They need no convincing that in the past there were people like them, souls who sought and found the truth, and expressed their findings under the name Kabbalah. It is natural for them to see this discipline and wisdom as the way that will help them find God.

For those seekers who did not recognize that Judaism possesses a soul, they now come to realize that they had been mistaken about what Judaism really is. They had not previously recognized that Judaism is a living organism possessing both body and soul.

In mainstream Judaism, there are many people who believe in, and are happy with, the body of the Torah, and that is very good, in and of itself. But if the Jews that have been distanced from the Torah and its commandments are to reclaim their Judaism, we must inspire them with a taste of truth so profound and sweet that they would never have thought exists within the framework of Judaism. Thus Kabbalah is often the best way to awaken Jewish souls to return to their true roots.

When coming back to Torah by way of Kabbalah, it is most important to study and receive the Kabbalah from an authentic source. Often, it is difficult to find an authentic source, whether teacher or institution of Kabbalah, which is geared to beginners. This is where the teachings of Chassidut fill the gap. For example, the Chassidic movement known as Chabad welcomes all beginners and offers teachings all of which are rooted in Kabbalah based on the model introduced by the Ba'al Shem Tov and developed further by the leaders of Chabad.

Classic Kabbalah discusses and analyzes in great detail the secrets of creation, some of which are extremely abstract. The application of those teachings to one's spiritual life is what Chassidut adds to the classic works of Kabbalah. Chassidut relates the secrets of creation to the mission of the soul on earth and to the moral and practical improvement of the human being (which in Kabbalah is called *tikun* or rectification). In our days it is best to begin the study of Kabbalah from the personal and inspiring perspective given by Chassidut.

The Book of Psalms states, "Taste and see how good is God."[10] When it comes to teaching Kabbalah, or indeed any topic, one has to first present a taste of the topic to the student. It is never sufficient to merely talk or write or read *about* something; a teacher of Kabbalah has to convey its inner wisdom so the student can taste it—that is, experience it. This means that Kabbalah must be presented authentically (in a manner completely faithful to the sources) on the one hand, while using idioms, language and experiential references that are appropriate for the audience. The teacher succeeds when the student is able not only to integrate the light, goodness, and sweetness of the Kabbalah, but also to convey it to others.

Approaching the Study of Kabbalah

There exist a number of introductory texts in English that aim to teach the secrets of Kabbalah. Unfortunately, not all of these can be considered reliable, and many are in fact misleading. However, when learning this or any other text in English, it should be remembered that the English translation of Hebrew (or Aramaic) terms can never be exact. The subtle meanings and inferences conveyed by these terms can only be grasped in the original Hebrew, which is the language of creation. Therefore, any serious student must realize that to go beyond a beginner's level, a mastery of the Hebrew language is essential.[11]

Beyond the question of terminology, difficulties may arise due to a basic difference between the approach to reading and study as practiced in Western culture and the different approach of the Torah and Kabbalah. Western culture sees the goal of study as the accumulation of knowledge, or, at least, the gleaning of information; whether skimming or reading, the intent is usually to take out the useful points and proceed further. In contrast, the Torah instructs us that the goal of study is the refinement of our behavior. Through our study we seek to come close to God, knowing that we can only draw close to Him by emulating His characteristics, as the sages say, "Just as God is merciful, so must you be merciful."[12]

As noted above, Kabbalah is first and foremost the study of God. When we delve into Divine mysteries and attributes with a completely sincere heart, day after day and hour after hour, we cannot help but refine our personalities in the process. This process also creates a feedback loop: the more that we study Kabbalah with the proper intent, the better we understand the manifestations of God in the world and seek to emulate His qualities. The more we refine our characters in emulation of God, the closer we come to the Divine Presence in creation and are thus better able to understand the inner dimension of reality and experience God in creation as revealed in our studies.

When our soul becomes one with mystical wisdom, our whole life pattern is changed—from the consciousness of our minds, to the emotions of our hearts, to every aspect of our behavior.

Most importantly, the study of Kabbalah depends upon the devotion and true desire of the heart of the student. This is a prerequisite—the true desire of the heart must be to come close to God. In addition, it depends upon revelation from above. Over the generations, more and more has been revealed. The ultimate revelation—which depends upon how truly we desire to come close to and become one with God—is the revelation prophesied for the Messianic Era, which as revealed by Chassidut, is imminent.

The Union of Kabbalah and Halachah

Another misconception that has unfortunately been spread in our generation is that Kabbalah is somehow a body of knowledge separate from the rest of the Torah. Kabbalah does not exist apart from the rest of the Torah. Indeed, as noted above, it is one aspect of the Torah, the body of the Torah being the law, and the soul of the Torah being Kabbalah. Just as it is impossible to imagine a soul without a body or a body without a soul as a functioning human being, so Kabbalah remains virtual and impotent without the study and practice of the legal aspects of the Torah. Ideally, serious students learn both the law of the Torah and Kabbalah simultaneously.

A body cannot live without a soul. The soul is sent from Above to enter the body, to cleave, in union, to the body in the mystery of life. In Kabbalah, the union of body and soul is called *Ma'aseh Merkavah*, the Workings of the Chariot, and is considered the deepest dimension of the Torah. In order to access this most secret of secrets—the mystery of the union of soul and body—one has to study both the soul and the body of the Torah.

Naturally, there are periods in life when one aspect of the Torah is emphasized more than the other. These are personal and particular issues for which no generic rules can be outlined. In general, for all, there has to be equilibrium, balance, and union. We have to devote ourselves to study the laws of the Torah and to comprehend the wisdom and reasoning behind the laws. Simultaneously, in order to meet God, the Giver of the laws, we have to study Kabbalah.

Study of the Torah restructures our thinking processes according to the God-given logic inherent in it. The Torah's innate thought-patterns, paradigms, and frames of reference become assimilated into our intellects and reflected in our lives.

Rather than proceeding in a linear fashion as is common in Western culture, the study of the Torah and Kabbalah proceeds in an associative and even circular fashion. One learns and then reviews again and again, each time adding a new, deeper layer of knowledge.

In this manner of study, the Written Torah, the Talmud, the codes of Jewish law, and Kabbalah, are seen as a single all-inclusive whole. No separation can be made between the legal dimensions of Torah study and practice—the *Halachah*, literally "the Way"—and its spiritual counterpart. The texts of Talmudic law are intrinsically united with the teachings of the Kabbalah. Similarly, Kabbalah cannot be studied without devotion to the Talmud, its commentaries, and the legal codes.

Thus, a student of Torah law must realize that an inner spiritual dimension exists in even the minutest aspect of Torah observance. Conversely, a student excited by the power of Kabbalah's spiritual teachings must realize that the fullest expression of these teachings comes in the day-to-day observance of the Torah's commandments.

Who Can Study Kabbalah?

Ideally, everyone should be able to study Kabbalah. Kabbalah is the inner wisdom of creation revealed to us by God in order to bring us closer to Him. Clearly, the Almighty desires that all human beings come as close to Him as possible. Thus, Kabbalah is important for all people.

That said, it is important to clarify that each of us has to study Kabbalah at his or her own individual level, which, contrary to common misconceptions, may have nothing to do with age, gender, or any other imagined limitation.

Even though there is an opinion that one should not begin to study Kabbalah until the age of 40, the great masters of Kabbalah and Chassidut did not agree with this opinion. Some of the greatest teachers of Kabbalah—including the Ari, Rabbi Moshe Chaim Luzzatto (also known as the Ramchal), and Rebbe Nachman of Breslov—did not even live to the age of 40! From an early age they began to study Kabbalah. In Kabbalah and Chassidut we find that a sign of the coming of the Messiah is young children studying and discussing the secrets of the Torah.[13]

The reasoning behind placing a limitation on the age at which it is appropriate to study Kabbalah was that until the age of 40 a person is not yet established or well-grounded. As the sages say, "At 40 years, a person gains understanding,"[14] a quality associated with the ability to serenely handle life's ups and downs. Or, in the words of those placing a minimum on the age, at the age of forty a person's blood has quieted, and he or she is no longer quick to get excited or treat things in an unbalanced, extreme manner. The attitude that the study of Kabbalah could (and should) be put-off until later in life implies that the inner wisdom of the Torah is merely a perk offered to those individuals who had already proven their worthiness.

However, over the years it has become apparent that without the study of the inner dimensions of the Torah as revealed through Kabbalah and Chassidut, there is very little chance that a person will ever reach a state of balance and inner calm.[15] The study of Kabbalah, especially through Chassidut, is no longer a luxury that a person can engage in once he or she has established him or herself, it has become a necessary part of the healthy intellectual, psychological, and behavioral development of every individual.

Chassidut reveals to us the drama of God's creation of the universe. It is like a game of hide-and-seek. In this Divinely inspired game, God conceals Himself, but He desires us to seek Him. He promises us that if we seek Him with all our heart and soul, we will ultimately find Him.

The seeking is the study of Kabbalah. It can begin from the first moment that a person realizes that there is more to this world than what meets the eye, and this can be at a very early stage of life.

Another reason that some authorities have warned against studying Kabbalah at too early an age was that there were instances in Jewish history, some relatively recent, when very negative phenomena resulted from the misrepesentation and misuse of Kabbalah. For example, in the 17th century, Shabbetai Tzvi (1626-1676) proclaimed himself the Messiah, basing his claim and his novel teachings on misinterpretations of Kabbalah. Before he was proven a fraud, he had brought great material and spiritual suffering to a significant portion of European Jewry.

This is one of the reasons that the Ba'al Shem Tov revealed a new dimension of Kabbalah. He expressed Kabbalah in a way that is accessible to every soul and that excludes all possibility of misinterpretation. This is another reason why it is highly recommended for beginning students of Kabbalah to start with the study of Chassidut. If one begins the study of Kabbalah properly, there is no danger. If there is no danger, there is also no age barrier or other limitation on the study of Kabbalah.

Indeed, the study of Kabbalah helps all fulfill the *Duties of the Heart* — the six constant commandments mandated by the Torah, which include the faith in God's Omnipresence and Providence over all, and love and awe of God.[16] These commandments are relevant to men, women, and children. Indeed, these commandments are a key factor in the education of children, as they form the foundation of a rectified state of consciousness, more easily formed when a child is young, and more difficult to attain in adulthood.

True experiences of faith, love, and awe depend upon the meditative process that comes with the study of the inner dimension of the Torah.

Maimonides—the great 11th century philosopher and codifier of the 613 commandments of the Torah—begins his classic work, the *Mishneh Torah*, with these commandments. He states that in order to attain love and awe of God as commanded in the Torah, one has to meditate upon the wonders of creation and the creative process. Maimonides lived before the revelation of the *Zohar*. Nonetheless, it was clear to him that every person is obligated to try and access the secrets of creation, because this is what strengthens one's faith in God and arouses in the heart the emotions of love and awe.[17]

Thus, if Kabbalah and Chassidut are studied for the sake of fulfilling the aforementioned *Duties of the Heart*, there is no difference between men and women, for these commandments are equally pertinent to all.

The study of the more technical sides of Kabbalah may not immediately produce the emotions of love and awe in the heart. However, this temporary lack is remedied by the study of Chassidic texts. As mentioned in the introduction, the *Tanya*, the seminal and classic text of Chassidut, brings down to earth the abstract and often impenetrable formulae of classical Kabbalah and translates them into the terms of ordinary human experience. Indeed, the explicit purpose of Chassidic texts is to arouse in the heart the emotions of love and awe.[18]

Of course, any subject must be studied at the level or degree of comprehension of the individual student. There are endless levels of understanding. One has to begin at the level relevant to him or her, and proceed from there.

Since Kabbalah is part of Jewish tradition, it is often mistakenly assumed that it has no pertinence to non-Jews. However, much of

Kabbalah is pertinent to all human beings, since the study of Kabbalah arouses in all students the desire to know and worship One God, as commanded in the Torah to all mankind.

Clearly, in order for non-Jews to study Kabbalah—which, after all, is an intrinsic expression of Jewish faith—they have to identify with receiving this wisdom through the channel of the Torah and the Jewish people, and commit themselves to worship the One God of Israel and live in accordance with the seven commandments given by Him to Noah for all peoples.[19]

Notes:

1. Abraham was born in the year 1948, i.e., 1948 years after the creation of the world. This year parallels the year 1812 BCE (Before the Common Era).

2. Emulating God's qualities and actions is a commandment in the Torah: "And you shall follow His ways." (Deuteronomy 28:9). Maimonides, the greatest codifier of the Torah's commandments, includes the commandment to emulate God as one of the 613 commandments of the Torah in his Book of Commandments (*Sefer Hamitzvot*, 8). See *The Art of Education* p. 133 and p. 140, n. 27.

3. See p. 21.

4. *Sefer Yetzirah* 1:1.

5. This terminology is found throughout Kabbalistic literature; Cf. *Zohar* III, 152a.

6. *Mishnah Chagigah* 1:8.

7. *Pesachim* 119a; *Chagigah* 13a and numerous times in the *Zohar*.

8. The sages say: "If the righteous would want, they could create a world" (*Sanhedrin* 65b). The "righteous" here refers to those holy individuals who have indeed merited purifying themselves and walking solely in the ways of the Almighty.

9. "Rabbi Elazar said: the light which God created on the first day, with it a person can see from one end of the universe to the other. When God saw the wicked deeds of the generation of the deluge, and of the generation of the tower of Babel, He concealed it. We learn this from the verse: '[He] prevented the wicked from

receiving their light' (Job 38:15) and who is He guarding it for? For the righteous; we learn this from the verse: 'God saw the light that it was goodly,' (Genesis 1:4) and the righteous are called goodly, as in the verse: 'proclaim that the righteous-one is good' (Isaiah 3:10)" (*Chagigah* 12a).

10. Psalms 34:9.

11. Indeed, there is an intrinsic connection between Kabbalah and the Hebrew language per se. In fact, the earliest text of Kabbalah, *Sefer Yetzirah,* is also the first text of Hebrew grammar.

12. *Jerusalem Talmud Pei'ah* 1:1 (3a).

13. See the Mittler Rebbe's *Torat Chaim, Shemot* 99b, and elsewhere.

14. *Mishnah Avot* 5:21.

15. In Chassidut, Kabbalah is symbolized by salt, which has the special quality of "sweetening the flesh" (*Berachot* 5a and Maharsha *Ibid.*), i.e., quieting the blood. See also Rabbi Shneur Zalman's *Likutei Torah Vayikra* 3d and following and the Tzemach Tzedek's *Or Hatorah Vayikra* pp. 226ff.

16. See p. 37ff.

17. *Mishneh Torah, Hilchot Yesodei Hatorah* 2:2.

18. See for example *Tanya,* chapter 16.

19. The seven commandments are known as the Noachide Laws; they are: prohibition against adultery, prohibition against murder, prohibition against theft, prohibition against idol worship, prohibition against blasphemy, prohibition against eating flesh from a live animal, and the obligation to establish a communal legal system. These commandments, their inner meaning, and the spiritual path of the non-Jew based on the Torah are discussed in depth in *Kabbalah and Meditation for the Nations.*

Contemplative vs. Practical Kabbalah

2

THERE ARE TWO BASIC TYPES OF KABBALAH:

♦ Contemplative Kabbalah (*Kabbalah iyunit*[1]), which seeks to explain the nature of God and the nature of existence via intellectual and meditative techniques, and

♦ Practical Kabbalah (*Kabbalah ma'asit*[2]), which seeks to alter the nature of existence and change the course of events via ritualistic techniques.

Although we will see that the distinction between contemplative Kabbalah and practical Kabbalah can often be quite arbitrary, the proper definition of these two types of Kabbalah will help us to better understand the mystical discipline of the Jewish people, its limitations, and ramifications.

Contemplative Kabbalah

To this category belong the majority of texts of Kabbalah in circulation (in print format) today. It sets out to explain the process whereby the created realm evolved into autonomous existence through the will of the infinite Creator; it elaborates as well upon the nature of the interaction between creation and the Divine source from which it emerges.

On an even deeper level, contemplative Kabbalah explores the complex nature of Divine reality itself—in particular, the paradox of God being immutable and yet active and reactive in His relationship with His creation.

The contemplative tradition also embraces various meditative techniques, often mistakenly identified with practical Kabbalah. These techniques are used to ponder the Divine subtext of reality and include the contemplation of Divine Names, of the various permutations of the letters of Hebrew words, and of the ways in which the ten *sefirot*—the manifestations of Divine light and energy—harmonize and interact. Some ancient forms of Kabbalistic meditation actually produce a visionary experience of higher spiritual chambers or worlds.

The worthy Kabbalist will surely draw light and blessing into our physical realm by means of meditation and concentrated focus on Divine unifications that take place in the higher worlds during the time of prayer. His prayers will be answered and the results manifest. He will change things for the better. This is not, however, practical Kabbalah. For indeed every good deed that every righteous individual—not just a Kabbalist—performs, in addition to having an immediate effect of drawing Divine energy into reality also changes the course of nature for the better.

Practical Kabbalah

This branch of Kabbalah uses the knowledge of Kabbalah in order to directly influence nature and human events. Sometimes this involves summoning spiritual forces and commanding them to act in reality through techniques such as the ritual incantation of Divine Names or the inscription of such Names (or names of angels) upon specially prepared amulets.

Because of its power for good and evil, *Kabbalah ma'asit* is to be employed by only the most holy and responsible of individuals and for no other purpose than the benefit of creation and the hastening of the realization of God's ultimate desire in creation.

The Arizal, whose teachings form the core of Kabbalistic doctrine today, exhorted his disciples to avoid the practical arts of Kabbalah (with the exception of writing amulets), for he deemed such practice forbidden in absence of the necessary state of ritual purity.[3]

When the Holy Temple stood in Jerusalem, it was possible for one to purify oneself (from the impurity that issues from contact with death) using the ashes of the red heifer.[4] At present we have neither the Temple nor the red heifer and are unable to purify ourselves as is necessary for the rituals of practical Kabbalah. When performed by a ritually impure person and without the level of holiness required, the arts of practical Kabbalah can be extremely detrimental to all involved. The Ari's prohibition in effect deferred the practice of practical Kabbalah to such a time as when the Temple will be rebuilt and the requisite state of purity once again attainable.

The Temple service was the primary framework within which the practical aspect of Kabbalah evolved. Whereas outside of the Temple service we are forbidden to actually pronounce God's essential Name, *Havayah*,[5] the rite of enunciating this Name, which was the centerpiece of the Temple service conducted by the High Priest on Yom Kippur, the Day of Atonement, was the source of the practical tradition in Kabbalah.[6] In addition, various other holy Names of God are reported to have been part of the priests' service in the Temple.[7]

Like other aspects of the practical tradition, the precise pronunciations and incantations of God's holy Names were passed down from generation to generation. Toward the end of the period of the Second Temple it was determined by the sages that, for fear of them being misused by the unworthy, these secrets should no longer be revealed—even in the Temple service the incantation of the Name was concealed in song—and after the destruction of the Temple they were purposefully forgotten.[8]

By concealing the precise pronunciation of God's Names, the sages provided a precedent for those who, like the Ari, argued in later generations against the practice of practical Kabbalah.

(Indeed, the Ari's fears proved to be well-founded as in the ensuing centuries we have witnessed the emergence of pseudo-Kabbalistic movements, driven by either rank opportunism or misguided spirituality, which by making use of pseudo-

Kabbalistic practical techniques compromised their followers' faith and well-being and in addition harmed the reputation of legitimate Kabbalistic pursuit.)

But there is more to be said regarding practical Kabbalah. Based on the principle set by the sages that often "the state of injury is indeed the remedy,"[9] the Ba'al Shem Tov saw that our present unworthiness to practice practical Kabbalah—that once found favor in the eyes of God when practiced by the worthy—is a sign from Heaven that we are now capable of reaching an even higher level of Divine service. He taught that the Jewish soul, "an actual part of God,"[10] possesses the power to influence reality and miraculously change the course of nature by means of simple faith, prayer to God, and good deeds.

Thus, the Ba'al Shem Tov taught that *there is no longer any need for practical Kabbalah!* The world at large, approaching the Messianic Age, has reached a higher potential state of consciousness. By connecting ourselves to the truly righteous individuals (*tzadikim*) of the generation—those souls whose consciousness is pure and holy, and in relation to whom our own souls are individual sparks—we can access the infinite resources of energy latent in our souls to work miracles.

In the future, with the coming of the Messiah and the building of the Temple, the miraculous will become natural and the esoteric will become common knowledge. We will then be pure in both body and spirit and God's ineffable Name will be an inseparable part of our natural everyday state of consciousness.

The Power of Simple Faith

Because the Jewish soul is "an actual part of God," its innate consciousness is known as *simple faith* (*emunah peshutah*) in God. This unity with God makes it possible for the soul to call upon the infinite power of the Almighty.[11] The following description and story exemplify the power of simple faith as taught by the Ba'al Shem Tov.[12]

> Rabbi Israel Ba'al Shem Tov did great things, the likes of which have not been seen or heard from the times of the holy *Tannaim* [sages of the Mishnah] Rabbi Shimon bar Yochai and Rabbi Chaninah ben Dosa and their contemporaries. And he did all this through his unshakable connection [dveikut] with the Almighty. And all this... he performed without a single holy Name, for all of his life he refrained from using holy Names.
>
> When he was still young, his teacher, Achiyah Hashiloni, had already taught him all of the holy Names and their use in order that he may understand and teach others. But once, when in danger, he placed a piece of cloth on the Dniester River and using a holy Name, used it to cross the river.
>
> He spent the rest of his life doing *teshuvah* [repentance] for this and fasted many times to try to remove the blemish.
>
> The end of his rectification came later in his life when once more he found himself being chased by bandits and to escape with his life needed to cross the Dniester. He placed his belt on the water and crossed the river without using any holy Names, but solely upon his great faith in the God of Israel.

When one repents truly and completely with all of one's heart, one receives a sign from heaven that the repentance has been accepted. One finds oneself in a situation similar to that of the original transgression, but this time, is able to act properly and pass the test.

The teachings of the Ba'al Shem Tov take the simple faith of every person to previously inexperienced heights. They advance Kabbalistic contemplation beyond the realm of philosophical abstraction and into the sphere of immediate psychological insight.

Wisdom and Prophecy

More so than the practical tradition of Kabbalah, the contemplative tradition of Kabbalah provides the optimal medium for attaining Divine enlightenment, while operating within the realm of the human intellect.

It is explained in Kabbalah that the capacity for inner reflection derives from the realm of souls, a realm that is hierarchically superior to the realm of angels[13] (the realm from which derive the exotic forces elicited through practical Kabbalah).

According to Kabbalah, the purpose of creation is to provide God with a "dwelling place in the lower realms."[14] Kabbalah seeks to achieve this by channeling Divine light into the progressively denser conduits of human thought, feeling, and deed, and from there into the rest of material reality. By working within the realm of human consciousness, the contemplative tradition sensitizes one to the infinite Divine nuance within creation. Though the Divine is ever-present in our lives, without training our minds through the study of Kabbalah to be sensitive to it, we essentially remain blind to It.

The elevation of thought to the point where it becomes a vessel worthy of inviting Divine wisdom and understanding constitutes the peak of spiritual accomplishment.

For this reason, Kabbalah sees wisdom as having an advantage over even such high states of enlightenment as prophecy; prophecy, by its very nature, *transcends* ordinary experience to reach the holy, while wisdom *elevates* ordinary experience *into* the realm of the holy. The advantage of wisdom over prophecy as a pathway to enlightenment is evident from the teaching of the sages that "the wise man is greater than the prophet."[15]

The prophetic experience, although extraordinarily vivid in its imagery, is divorced from normative here-and-now sensual experience and thus remains essentially impenetrable and enigmatic to others. Through prophecy we may arrive at the ultimate approximation of Divine thought, but without necessarily impacting the self or creation as a whole. Wisdom, on the other hand, serves to translate our deepest experiences of God and the world into the terminology of ordinary consciousness that can be conveyed and understood by others.

The only individual for whom wisdom and prophecy merged into a single stream of enlightenment was Moses.[16] He was able to receive prophecy while still in full possession of his normative human faculties, thereby providing the quintessential model of rectified consciousness. He was both the wisest of men and the most Divinely attuned—the greatest of prophets; the only human being who could, as it were, meet God half-way up the mountain.

The Kabbalistic tradition, though grounded in the prophetic experience of the patriarchs and sages, has moved steadily over time in the direction of conveying its wisdom to progressively wider circles of recipients. This is part of a providential plan that sees the greatest benefit to God (in His desire that we sustain Him, as it were) and creation in the cultivation of a spiritual consciousness firmly grounded within physical reality. This plan is evident from numerous references in the Bible; for example Isaiah states:

> ... the earth shall be full of the knowledge of God as the waters cover the sea... eye to eye, they shall see the returning of God to Zion... [17]

Kabbalah, as the framework within which Jews have historically evolved their unique understanding of reality, represents both a legacy of prophecy and of wisdom. This is portrayed vividly in *gematria,* the system of calculating numerical values of Hebrew words and thus discerning their deeper meaning.[18] The numerical value of the Hebrew word "Kabbalah" (קַבָּלָה), 137, is equal to the sum of the values of the two words "wisdom" (חָכְמָה), 73, and "prophecy" (נְבוּאָה), 64.[19]

Through the wisdom of Kabbalah, we learn to hear that which the Israelites saw at Mt. Sinai.[20] Once we fully comprehend the conceptual significance of that vision, we will once again begin to see God, but with our natural senses intact, and not only for the moment, but for all time thereafter.

Kabbalistic Meditation

As Kabbalah sees it, our mind is the interface between our soul and reality. We are constantly being bombarded with stimuli and sensations from the world outside ourselves; the mind processes this onrush of sensations and determines which are to be taken note of and then sorts and prioritizes them and finally decides what response is appropriate to what stimulus, based on past experiences or principles.

The way our mind functions, then, is what determines how we relate to our environment. To take full advantage of our time, we must provide our mind with proper categories with which to process reality, think about it and relate to it.

Providing us with the most useful and practical categories is a fundamental goal of Jewish meditation in accordance with Kabbalah. Through meditation, we take the untamed mind and train it to think in terms of images that are true and based on the Torah. By taking a subject through deeper and deeper levels of abstraction, we reach and affect deeper and deeper dimensions of our mind, and thus gradually change ourselves and the way we respond to the world around and within us.

To this end, the seasoned meditator will make use of the whole range of Biblical, Talmudic, Midrashic, Kabbalistic, Rabbinic, Chassidic, and Jewish philosophical and ethical literature. The wisdom contained in all these sources serves to fertilize the potent ground of his imagination and faculty of association and produces a conceptual garden of ever-evolving multi-dimensional insights into reality. Furthermore, when evaluated in a Torah context, empirical information from nature can also be summoned to the same end.

Meditation is in-depth contemplation of concepts and truths, in order to thoroughly understand the concepts themselves and establish points of application between them and one's personal life. Meditation is enhanced by speaking or hearing the words of the Torah (if possible in the original Hebrew, the language of creation) and simultaneously envisioning the letters, counting them as if they were precious jewels.

According to Kabbalah, when we meditate properly, our hearts are aroused to turn away from physical pursuits, egotistic considerations, and the deceit and emptiness that normally plague our lives. We turn away from these illusory states of existence and turn toward the one true reality—God.

As is the case with regard to all human endeavors, the successful effectiveness of any meditation is clearly a gift from God. However, we are all granted free choice, which we must utilize maximally in order to merit the gift of God's response. In the case of meditation, we search for God from the depths of our hearts and He allows us to find Him.

Many beginners mistakenly think of meditation as an attempt to negate and thereby transcend one's normative thought process. This is often the case with those who have been exposed to impure meditative practices originating with religions rooted in idolatry or paganism or associated with the denial of the existence of God.

Kabbalistic meditation, however, is not a negation or destruction, rather it is a construction. In fact the Hebrew word for "meditation," *hitbonenut*, stems from the Hebrew root which means "to build."[21]

Here is one example of a Kabbalistic meditation, the subject of an entire volume,[22] which illustrates how this process works. Those who have been exposed to other practices will immediately perceive the difference.

This meditation consists of constructing an imaginary meditative space in the shape of a cube around oneself—a protective sanctuary in which one is able to pray, that is, engage in active dialogue with God.

The six faces or walls of this spiritual sanctuary are meditatively constructed from the six continuous *Duties of the Heart* mentioned above,[23] which are:

- belief in God's existence and providence
- not to believe that there are any other gods
- to believe that God is absolutely One
- to love God
- to fear God
- to shield one's mind from negative influence

When utilized as the walls of our sanctuary, these commandments create the space in which constant conscious awareness of God can be maintained.

To begin this mediation, we imagine ourselves in a sanctuary whose ceiling is the presence of God (1), whose floor is the negation of belief in any other gods (2), whose front is the absolute unity of God (3), whose right side is the love of God (4), whose left side is the fear of God (5), and whose back is the sentry against negative thoughts (6).

The order of this meditation follows the logic of cause and effect: we first become aware that God exists; this leads us to deny all other pseudo-deities. Once that is done, we see God in everything (and as everything). This leads us to love God, and our love brings us to fear separation from Him. This fear in turn inspires us to defend ourselves from distracting or confusing influences.

Once the mental sanctuary has been built and the concepts are well understood, the classic method for ongoing meditation is to reflect on it before prayer, trying to sense or contact the Divinity pervading these concepts, and using them as a method of enhancing our ever-unfolding and developing face-to-face relationship with the Almighty.

But building consists of more than a skeletal frame. Ultimately, Kabbalistic meditation means adding layers upon layers of elaboration and meaning with which to strengthen and embellish the basic structure. Each level of meditation adds in its own way to the overall potential of the meditation or the appreciation of its astounding beauty—which, of course, implies a heightened appreciation for the beauty of the Torah itself—both of which serve to increase the meditation's potency in affecting our soul, our mind, and our life in general.

Notes:

1. The Hebrew word *iyunit*, which is usually translated as contemplative, literally means "with the eye," referring to what is known as the mind's eye. Deep contemplation requires that the object of contemplation become visible to the mind's eye. If this does not occur then a person's understanding of the topic is still lacking. The most basic object of continuous contemplation is God's essential four-letter Name, *Havayah*, as stated in Psalms, "I place *Havayah* before me always" (16:8). The word *Havayah* is actually a permutation of the four letters that make up the Name itself, which we are forbidden to pronounce as written. Permuted in this way to spell *Havayah*, the four letters of God's essential Name mean "existence," alluding to the fact that "God is all [of existence]" and that God continuously brings all of reality into existence *ex nihilo*. This is what the contemplative eye of the meditator focuses on seeing.

2. The Talmud relates that Rava created a man. He sent it to Rabbi Zeira who spoke to it, but it did not respond. He said to it: "You have been created by our friends. Return to your earth." Rav Chaninah and Rav Oshayah would sit down every Saturday night and study *Sefer Yetzirah*. They then created a large calf which they ate (*Sanhedrin* 65b).

3. The state of ritual purity required can only be achieved by administering the ash of the red heifer, which the sages tell us will be produced again with the coming of the Messiah. See next note. Much of the Ari's rationale on this subject appears in his disciple's Rabbi Chayim Vital's volume *Sha'arei Kedushah* (Gates of Holiness).

4. The red heifer as a form of ritual purification from the profane (*tum'ah*) is prescribed by the Torah. See Numbers chapter 19.

5. See note 1.

6. *Yoma* 39b.

7. For instance the Name of 12 letters, which is discussed in the Talmud (*Kidushin* 71a).

8. *Ibid.*

9. "*Kalkalato takanato,*" see *Shulchan Aruch Even Ha'ezer* 173:1 and elsewhere.

10. *Tanya,* beginning of chapter 2, based on Job 31:2.

11. See for instance the Lubavitcher Rebbe's *Hayom Yom,* for the 11th day of Tishrei: "Prayer with simple faith connects the essence of the soul with the Almighty Himself, causing God Himself to be 'the healer of the sick' and 'the one who blesses the year.'"

12. See Rabbi Yitzchak Isaac Safrin (the Komarna Rebbe), *Notzer Chesed al Masechet Avot,* 6, *Ahavah* §8. See also Rabbi Moshe Cha'im of Sdilkov, *Degel Machaneh Efra'im, Vayishlach,* "*Ki bemakli.*"

13. Invariably, man is considered to be dynamic and the angles static, as in the verse "I will give you [Joshua, the High Priest] dynamic walkers among these standers [angels]" (Zachariah 3:7), or in the verse "and all the hosts of heaven stand before Him" (II Chronicles 18:18, I Kings 22:19); see also *Zohar* III, 260a.

14. *Midrash Tanchuma, Naso* 16 (ed. Buber 24).

15. *Bava Batra* 12a, based on the verse "… and the heart of the prophet is wise" (Psalms 90:12).

16. Moses was the greatest of all prophets and experienced prophecy in a different manner than all the others because of the marriage of wisdom and prophecy in him; See Maimonides *Hilchot Yesodei Hatorah* 7:6; *Commentary on the Mishnah,* "Introduction to *Perek Chelek,*" 7th principle; and, Introduction to *Guide to the Perplexed* and *Ibid.* II, 35 (see also ch. 36).

17 Isaiah 11:9, 52:8.

18. For more on *gematria* and its origins, see the entry "gematria" in the Glossary.

19. The initial letters of prophecy (נ) and wisdom (נ) in Hebrew spell the word חן, which is also a popular acronym that stands for "inner wisdom," one of the names of Kabbalah. These two letters

are also an acronym for the impure and immodest sexual conduct exercised in youth, implying that the study of Kabbalah heals one from the blemish of these sins.

137 is considered one of the most astonishing numbers in modern physics, as it is the inverse of the fine structure constant. It is also the numerical value of the Hebrew word אוֹפָן (pronounced: *ofan*), literally "wheel," referring to a type of angel (described in Ezekiel, chapter 1). Because of physical considerations relating the electron (understood in modern physics not to be a "thing," but rather a "wheel" of energy) with the fine structure constant (the ratio of the speed of light to the speed of the electron), we define אוֹפָן (*ofan*) as the correct Hebrew name of the electron.

20. Exodus 20:15.

21. In *A Pamphlet on Prayer* (*Kuntres Hatfilah*), Rabbi Shalom Dov Ber Schneersohn, the fifth Lubavitcher Rebbe, explains the ramifications of the common etymological root of meditating and building. Before constructing a building it is necessary to clear the ground. Likewise, before meditating it is necessary to clear the ground, that is, the mind, from all distracting thoughts.

22. See *Living in Divine Space: Kabbalah and Meditation*.

23. Of the 613 commandments in the Torah, only these six are applicable to every Jew at every waking moment. These six constant commandments are brought down in both the introduction to *Sefer Hachinuch* and in the *Mishnah Berurah, Biur Halachah* on the opening statement of the *Rama* on the *Shulchan Aruch* 1:1. For a full treatment of the six constant commandments and how they form the basis of Jewish consciousness, see *Living in Divine Space: Kabbalah and Meditation*.

The Misuse of Kabbalah 3

THE POWER OF THE SOUL TO AFFECT EVENTS IN OUR WORLD, NOT necessarily by means of practical Kabbalah, is called *conscious determination*. This power of the soul originates in one's *simple* and *absolute faith* in God's essence as taught by the Ba'al Shem Tov and as discussed at the end of the previous chapter. Simple faith is strengthened and brought to the foreground of one's consciousness by the inspiration that comes from the true study of Kabbalah. When God's light penetrates and permeates the soul, it imbues one with the power to project one's simple faith, via the processing faculties of will and intellect, into one's surroundings, thereby affecting actual physical events in the real world.

The power of conscious determination is greatly misunderstood and at times misused. We will examine here some issues, of which the beginning student of Kabbalah must be aware so as not to stumble into practices entailing spiritual impurity and darkness.

Healing with Kabbalah

Because some great Kabbalists of the past were known as healers, there exists a great deal of confusion regarding the use of Kabbalah to access spiritual healing powers.

In general, unless the healer is a true *tzadik*—a holy and righteous individual—his healing or psychic powers are always a mixture of light and darkness, good and evil, in unknown proportions. When good and evil, or truth and falsehood, are mixed together, the final result is usually negative. Thus, it is better to stay clear of these practices lest one be irreparably harmed by them.

However, it is permissible to use the letters of the Hebrew alphabet to focus the intentions of one's prayers in order to heal. For example, the letter *tet* is known to correspond in Kabbalah to the left kidney;[1] it is therefore permissible to meditate on the letter *tet* while praying to God, the true Healer, to heal this organ of the body. One may even pray to God that healing energy be channeled and projected by the letter *tet* to the ailing person. This, of course, does not preclude the possibility that sincere prayer to God will not help as well or even more without this Kabbalistic knowledge and focus. This is a most individual matter, and only a mature, sensitive soul, a true servant of God, knows whether or not it is advisable for him to include such thoughts in his prayers. In any case, under no circumstances should this form of healing be given a foreign name, such as "Jewish reiki," as this involves linking a holy practice with idol worship and turns its power to evil. Great harm can come from such mixing.

Many of the great *tzadikim* of the past who possessed supernatural powers in their youth later abandoned them. In hindsight they related that when they arrived at a certain maturity of understanding in their study of the Torah in general and Kabbalah in particular, they came to see the use of those powers as actually detrimental to their own progress in the service of God and to their ability to *truly* help others. Thus they asked God to take these powers from them.

At the beginning of his public life, the Ba'al Shem Tov, who was a healer, used amulets (to be worn by the recipient for protection and healing); but, later he abandoned the practice. Even when writing an amulet, he would not inscribe holy Names of God but only sign his own signature, thereby radiating blessing directly from his own soul.[2]

In our own generation, every Sunday, Rabbi Menachem Mendel Schneersohn, the Lubavitcher Rebbe, would hand out dollar bills to thousands of people, so that they might give them to charity. His actions were based on the teachings of the sages of the

Talmud that whoever receives money from the hands of a *tzadik* receives a blessing.[3]

Using Kabbalah to Predict the Future

In every generation there are true *tzadikim* that possess *ru'ach hakodesh*, literally, "sacred spirit." Surely, the devoted study of Kabbalah helps make them worthy to receive this gift. These *tzadikim* are able to read the minds of others and to intuit future events. They generally attempt to hide what they know by *ruach hakodesh* or to disguise it in the garb of common intelligence.

Foreseeing and taking into consideration the consequences of one's deeds is the proper way to live. The sages teach that: "Who is wise? He who foresees the results of his deeds."[4] On the other hand, using the wisdom of Kabbalah to predict the future, by whatever form of esoteric logic or manipulation, is strictly forbidden by Jewish law. It borders on the practice of magic.[5]

Furthermore, many misconceptions exist about the connection between Kabbalah and astrology, tarot cards, heavenly portents, and the numerology of proper names. We shall try to briefly clarify what some of these practices are and identify those which are considered credible and those which are considered idol worship, magic, or just plain nonsense.

In its analysis of the ten *sefirot* (the ten Divine emanations of creative energy) and the twenty-two Hebrew letters, *Sefer Yetzirah* draws the correspondence between a subset of twelve letters of the Hebrew alphabet[6] to the twelve signs of the zodiac, the twelve months of the year, the twelve tribes of Israel, and the twelve senses of the soul.[7] These correspondences withstanding, the Talmud teaches that "Israel is above the influence and forecasts of the signs of the zodiac."[8] Therefore the study of astrology with the aim of anticipating or predicting the future is totally futile for a Jew. Knowing the signs of the zodiac and their correspondences may only be helpful in recognizing one's natural proclivities or innate character traits, which may be changed (even to the very opposite extremity) by our power of free choice.

According to 12th century philosopher and astronomer, Rabbi Abraham Ibn Ezra, who unlike Maimonides gave a certain amount of credence to astrology, the sign of the zodiac which most reflects the innate character-traits of the Jewish people is Aquarius, the water carrier.[9]

Though the hippies of the 1960s heralded the coming of world peace with the phrase "this is the dawning of the Age of Aquarius" because of some astrological reasoning, it was not a coincidence. Judaism identifies world peace with the Messianic age, a time when the prophecies of Isaiah will be fulfilled:

> And they shall beat their swords into plowshares and their spears into pruning hooks; nation shall not lift up sword against nation. Neither shall they learn war anymore... [At that time] the wolf shall dwell with the lamb, the leopard lie down with the kid, the calf and the beast of prey shall feed together with a little child to herd them.[10]

The dawning of the Messianic age will occur when the Torah and the Jewish people will finally recognize themselves and be recognized by others as the "light unto the nations"[11]—it will then truly be the Age of Aquarius.

With that said, it is important to stress that astrology is not a healthy interest for either a Jew or a non-Jew. The essential article of faith common to all human beings is the belief in one God and no other. Although the study of astrology does not necessarily constitute a breach of that faith, it can lead those who study it to ascribe inordinate power and significance to the heavenly bodies that God set in the firmament—thereby creating fertile ground for consequent inappropriate expressions of worship. Indeed, the common term used in Talmudic sources to denote a pagan is *akum*, a Hebrew acronym for one who worships the stars and zodiacal signs.

A dubious practice that unfortunately is quite popular in some circles is that of a prospective couple consulting a so-called "Kabbalist" to determine if theirs is a proper match—in other words, if their marriage will succeed. The "Kabbalist" typically performs various calculations of the numerical values of the couple's names and advises them to marry or not to marry.

Though such "Kabbalists" will often claim that they are engaging in practical Kabbalah, in truth this type of fortune-telling is neither practical Kabbalah nor is it in any way significant. It should not be pursued or requested.

Certainly, once a couple makes a decision to marry, a genuine Kabbalist can help them to understand the meanings of their names, their relation to one another, and other facets of the significance of their union. But, none of these can or should undermine (or catalyze) the couple's decision, which should be arrived on solely based on their sense of spiritual, intellectual, and emotional affinity. The key element in a successful marriage is the trust that both put in the Divine sanctity of their union, and the love that grows out of a joint commitment to building a healthy, loving, pure, and sanctified home in which the Divine Presence can dwell.[12]

A genuine Kabbalist is a holy person who, in his quest to find God and come close to Him, has developed spiritually and has been gifted with acute spiritual senses. Such a person can certainly be approached and consulted regarding any and all life questions because he is connected to the inner study of Kabbalah and has a deep understanding of the soul. He is able to sense reality on a deeper plane than the average individual, and knows, in all honesty, if, when, and what to recommend to every person that approaches him. The guiding principle of every genuine Kabbalist is making the world a better place by bringing people closer to God and hence to one another. A Kabbalist will never act or speak in a pre-meditated way with the purpose of tearing a sanctified union apart, or to cause argument or pain. Instead, he will always search for ways to bring people closer together and alleviate suffering and separateness.

Averting the Dangers of Kabbalah

Before learning Kabbalah it is necessary that precautions be taken to ensure that the highly energetic (psychological) and consciousness altering (spiritual) power of this part of the Torah not cause more damage than good. While many of the psychological dangers[13] are no longer so much of an issue, spiritual dangers that place a person's spiritual and consequently physical well-being in jeopardy still exist.

The first danger lies in the notion that it is possible to study Kabbalah without performing commandments. We have stressed a number of times that Kabbalah is the outcome of the mystical union between the spirit of prophecy and the tradition of *Halachah*. The attempt to have mystical experiences (even prophetic ones) without creating the proper vessels to contain them is hazardous because it is like creating a soul without a body and ultimately can lead to the soul leaving the body prematurely. The Torah's commandments give life,[14] that is, they make life possible by forming the vessels within which the soul resides.

The Torah tells us of great souls, like the two eldest sons of Aaron (Moses' brother, and the High Priest) Nadav and Avihu, who were deeply immersed in the most profound mysteries of the Divine, yet, because they did not perform a commandment of God, perished while serving in the Tabernacle.[15] In Kabbalah, their mistake is described as a "run without return"—an overly enthusiastic ascent to G-d without a proper anchor provided by the performance of commandments; an anchor that ensures that the person remains grounded, even while ascending to the highest levels of spirituality.

A genuine teacher of Kabbalah must never give a student the false conception that commitment to the Torah as a whole (613 commandments for a Jew and 7 for a non-Jew) is not required by someone wishing to learn Kabbalah. Nonetheless, the teacher has to know how to properly take the risk of bringing someone who is not yet ready to commit to the Torah as a whole, closer to the Almighty and His Torah by introducing him to the Torah's soul.

The second danger lies with who one chooses to learn Kabbalah from. Even when willing to or already living according to the Torah one may be receiving wisdom from an unauthentic source. Apart from the outright charlatans and those not well versed in the classic texts of Kabbalah, there are teachers who though they may mean well and are knowledgeable to a certain degree in Kabbalah, are actually ignorant when it comes to the rest of the Torah. As much as the logic in Kabbalah and Chassidut is super-rational, even the super-rational is preceded by the rational—the logic of the revealed part of the Torah. When knowledge of the revealed is lacking, a person cannot possibly understand or teach others the Torah's concealed facets; consequently, whether consciously or unconsciously, they teach incorrect knowledge.

Even if one finds an authentic source in a teacher who is learned both in the revealed and concealed aspects of the Torah there is still one more danger, more subtle, yet usually the one that most people end up being harmed by. Many of the teachers of Kabbalah only understand its external, technical aspects, but are completely lacking an understanding of its inner message. Inner understanding of Kabbalah means being able to experience the teachings in a rectified and holy manner (both on the intellectual as well as the emotional plane) and to transfer that experience and its meaning to students. An authentic teacher of Kabbalah understands and relays to his students that Kabbalah is not referring solely to external reality or external mystical experiences. The previous Lubavitcher Rebbe, Rabbi Yosef Yitzchak Schneersohn, said something very important in this respect: if a person gets used to looking at and experiencing the world externally, not only is he temporarily unaware of inner reality but he is even liable to injure his or her ability to later acquire an inner perspective on the world. Without an inner perspective the study of Kabbalah can deteriorate into a corporealization of God, which is forbidden. (It can further deteriorate into the self-worship-like gratification that comes with pseudo-mystical experience.) Throughout the generations, this has been the most problematic and the most feared consequence of the improper study of

Kabbalah. Rabbi Shimon bar Yochai begins one of the deepest sections of the *Zohar*, the *Idra Rabbah*, with the verse "Cursed is the man who makes an idol or a molten image... and sets it up in secret,"[16] a clear reference to the danger of corporealization (*hagshamah*) inherent in studying the "secrets" of the Torah.

To avert this final danger the Ba'al Shem Tov prescribed that Kabbalah should be studied only through the lens of Chassidut. Even when the classic texts of Kabbalah (that predate Chassidut) are studied with a heart for inner understanding, nonetheless, because of the coarseness of the human mind, the teachings may be misinterpreted and the result may be an anthropomorphization of the Almighty.[17]

The internal spiritual work needed to avert these three dangers corresponds to the three stages of all transformation taught by the Ba'al Shem Tov and discussed in length elsewhere.[18] They are: submission, separation, and sweetening. To avert the first danger one needs to submissively acknowledge that action must come before understanding[19] and that in order to study Kabbalah there must be a commitment to the Torah as a whole. Averting the danger of being seduced by an unauthentic source requires us to distance ourselves from unworthy teachers, no matter how promising they seem. Separation from that which is negative leads to a strengthening of our true identity and an ability to define our goals more precisely. Finally, studying Kabbalah from the perspective offered by the teachings of the Ba'al Shem Tov only requires that one have a proverbial sweet tooth for the inner sweetness of the Torah and its hidden dimensions.

Confusing Kabbalah with Eastern Religions

The Book of Genesis relates that, following the death of Sarah, Abraham remarried and fathered more children:

> To the sons of the concubines that Abraham had, he gave gifts. He sent them away from Isaac, his son, while he was still alive. He sent them eastward to the Land of the East.[20]

This passage has led some to claim that Eastern religious practices and healing methods are based on the ancient teachings of Abraham—the gifts that he gave his offspring whom he sent to the Land of the East—and that therefore they are related in some way to Judaism, which Abraham as the first patriarch of the Jewish people, passed on to Isaac. Somehow, this line of reasoning is used to legitimize the interest and even practice of Eastern religions by Jews.

However, this passage from Genesis clearly states that Abraham wanted to send his younger offspring "away from Isaac." Because Isaac was the sole inheritor of Abraham's holy mission to spread the knowledge of the One God, Abraham distanced the foreign children of his concubines because they practiced idolatry in order to prevent them from influencing Isaac.

So, even if the spiritual practices of the East that are known today do indeed originate with the sons of Abraham—which is highly doubtful—they are contaminated with idolatry and are considered spiritually impure and forbidden. As noted earlier, mixing anything that is spiritually impure with that which is spiritually pure has negative results and can be seriously harmful, both physically and spiritually.

This is not to say that there is no wisdom in foreign spiritual practices. Indeed, it is true that everything in this world—including evil—would not exist if it did not have a spark of holiness trapped within it from which it draws life energy. It is our mission in life to liberate these fallen sparks scattered throughout reality, especially in the garb of impure spiritual practices.

The sages teach, "Believe that there is *wisdom* from a non-Jewish source, [but] do not believe that there is *Torah* from a non-Jewish source."[21] The wisdom of which the sages speak refers to the holy sparks of truth that are trapped in the secular arts, sciences, and foreign spiritual practices and philosophies. Of course, before the wisdom can be trusted, the holy sparks must be liberated from the shells of impurity and idolatry, in which they are lodged and trapped. All beliefs must concur with the belief in the One God of

Israel and His Torah. To liberate the sparks requires one to be able to identify the true source of the trapped wisdom. That true source is the Torah.

The Torah is a complete way of life and is therefore called "the Torah of life."[22] The injunction "do not believe that there is Torah from a non-Jewish source," means that there is no true way of life, for any people or individual, other than that of the Torah. The Torah that was given to the world through the nation of Israel at Mt. Sinai is God's blueprint of creation. Its 613 commandments for Jews and 7 commandments for non-Jews are the sole prescription for how to live a full and rectified life. The sparks of wisdom present in non-Jewish sources must be brought under the wings of the faith of Israel; they must first be returned to their true source, the Torah. In other words, they must first undergo an intellectual conversion of sorts.

In general, the names by which foreign practices and philosophies refer to themselves are not meaningless; they indicate the faux "Torah," which they have invented. As such, it is forbidden to adopt such a name, even in an apparently Jewish context. As mentioned above, one must not practice or even speak of Jewish reiki, Jewish yoga, Jewish tai chi, or the like. Each of these names (reike, yoga, etc.) carries a particular impure power and is a source of confusion. Linking the Torah with a name rooted in idol worship or even in secular philosophy, turns its power to evil, making it most dangerous and strictly forbidden. As noted earlier, only harm can come from such mixing.

Taking symbols or images from these sources is also extremely dangerous. For example, the Chinese symbols used in reiki are definite tools of idol worship and may not be used. A symbol is like a name; if it derives from an impure source it carries with it impure energy. It is not like a point or spark of wisdom that may be liberated and converted completely to Judaism.

✿

Let us offer an example of a true intellectual conversion process. We learn in Kabbalah that there are fifteen contact points or energy centers down the middle line of the body. To one familiar with yoga, the seven chakras immediately come to mind.

The first stage of the conversion process is to take care not to confuse the two concepts. The belief in chakras as the body's energy centers, as taught in yoga, derives from an impure, foreign source, and, as a complete system, is false.

The second stage of the conversion process begins with the realization that although all of the spiritual and physical properties attributed to the chakras by yoga are certainly not true, there may be points of wisdom that one has gained from the study of chakras. These points of wisdom may be converted to Judaism. But, in order to do so they must be totally disassociated from their impure source and not called by their foreign name, just as a true convert to Judaism must totally disassociate from his past.

Thereafter, one may proceed to the third and final state of the conversion process—the recognition of the true source of the seven points and their functions in the complete, rectified system of the fifteen contact points described in Kabbalah. Now one may fully *believe* in the newly redeemed wisdom that had previously been trapped in a foreign shell.

Let us note that the three stages of the conversion process just described correspond to the three stages of the paradigmatic process of rectification taught by the Ba'al Shem Tov: submission, separation, and sweetening.[23] Knowing that the chakras derive from an impure source is submission. Disassociating the points of wisdom from their source is separation. Incorporating the points of wisdom in the complete system of the fifteen contact points, as taught in Kabbalah, is sweetening.[24]

Finally, let us say a word about Eastern meditation. Eastern forms of meditation pose very serious problems for the seeker of truth, and are strictly forbidden. The mantras used in Eastern meditation are for the most part names of idols or false gods. The entire system draws its energy from an impure source that creates in the psyche—by the endless repetition of a mantra that numbs the true inner senses of the soul—a false sense of negating the ego, antithetically opposed to the true sense of selflessness, *bitul,* characteristic of Judaism in general and of Jewish meditation in particular.

Reincarnation

Many books have been written explaining the teachings of the Ari on the subject of reincarnation (*gilgulim* or *gilgul neshamot*). These books explain when, and how, reincarnation takes place and give details regarding many soul-roots and how we find them reincarnated in the Bible and afterwards in the time of the sages, and even up to the time of the Ari himself.

The Ari traced the *gilgulim* of archetypal souls from Adam to his own generation and explained that in addition to the purpose of rectifying blemishes of previous lifetimes, each successive incarnation is in order to manifest and rectify a new, different dimension of the same soul.

According to the teachings of the Ari, Adam becomes David who will finally be reincarnated as the Messiah, as indicated by the fact that in Hebrew, Adam (אָדָם) comprises three letters, which are the initial letters of the three names: Adam (אָדָם), David (דָּוִד), and Messiah (מָשִׁיחַ). All were contained within the soul of Adam. Similarly, the three letters that comprise the name Moses (משה) are the initials of the three names Moses (מֹשֶׁה), Seth (שֵׁת), Abel (הֶבֶל), the three primary incarnations of this archetypal soul from future to past.

The Ari was able to reveal to his disciples their past incarnations so that they would be able to rectify the blemishes of the previous lifetimes in this one and continue to reach new and higher levels of consciousness.

According to the Ba'al Shem Tov, it is not necessary to reveal this information to every individual. Sometimes knowing our past life history can be detrimental to our rectification in this life. This knowledge can confuse the mind and not allow us to be open to achieve good in a simple and pure fashion; thus, that kind of knowledge can narrow our consciousness as opposed to broadening it. As noted above regarding the lack of purity that prevents us from engaging in practical Kabbalah, many times *that which damages is itself the remedy*. Whereas in previous generations knowledge of one's previous soul-lives may have been necessary to promote change, in our generation that we are born unaware of these soul-lives is actually a blessing. Because of the nature of modern life, not knowing about past soul-lives is actually liberating and promotes in us a feeling of greater freedom of choice.

In any case, it is important to understand that in Judaism reincarnation is in no way cruel or fatalistic, as it is in the teachings of Eastern philosophies. In the East, people suspend compassion, allowing their fellow human beings to die of disease and starvation in the streets, on the pretext that such suffering is one's just due for past-life sins. In contrast, Judaism instructs us to always be concerned to change the reality (the present moment) of this world for the better. For a Jew, the world in which we live exists and has meaning and purpose. Indeed, all of the worlds were created for the sake of this world, in order that by our good deeds we make this lowest realm of existence a dwelling place for the Almighty. Every successive incarnation is another chance, which benefits from new input of Divine energy, to succeed in one's holy mission on earth. In the end we will all succeed, and in the present helping each other succeed is an intrinsic part of one's own success.

Notes:

1. *Sefer Yetzirah* 5:2. For a more complete discussion of the various correspondences between Kabbalistic conceptual schemes and human physiology, see *Body, Mind, and Soul*.
2. See chapter 2, note 13 regarding the superiority of the soul to any angel or force that can be summoned to act.
3. See *Bava Batra* 15b: "Anyone who took charity from Job was blessed."

4. *Tamid* 32a.

5. Deuteronomy 18:9-12.

6. See p. 70ff.

7. *Sefer Yetzirah,* Chapter 5.

8. *Shabbat* 156a.

9. Commentary to Exodus 31:18.

10. Isaiah 2:4, 11:6.

11. Ibid. 42:6, 49:6.

12. For more on creating a successful marriage based on these principles, see *The Mystery of Marriage: How to Find Love and Happiness in Married Life.*

13. Past experience provides many examples of people who lost their mind, or were psychologically hurt from studying Kabbalah in an inappropriate manner. Most of these individuals were not entirely stable to start with, nonetheless, there is no question that the improper study of Kabbalah contributed to some extent to their psychological breakdown.

14. Leviticus 18:5.

15. Ibid. ibid.:10

16. Deuteronomy 27:15.

17. The teachings of Kabbalah involve a personification of the Divine. This is especially true of the teachings of the Arizal where the Divine is described by an entire sequence of interlocking personas, which we will discuss in part II. Consider the secret of the contraction (*tzimtzum*), the first topic discussed in the Arizal's writings. If one understands this secret literally, one may come to the conclusion that God is not omnipresent in reality; that somehow "God has left the earth" (Ezekiel 8:12) and receded from it. Only by studying the teachings of Chassidut are we convinced that the contraction of God's light is not literal but metaphorical.

18. See *Transforming Darkness Into Light: Kabbalah and Psychology.*

19. As stated by the Jewish people prior to making a covenant with God for receiving the Torah: "We shall do and [then] we shall hear [i.e., understand]" (Exodus 24:7).

20. Genesis 25:6.

21. *Midrash Eichah Rabbati* 2:13.

22. Final benediction of the *Amidah*.

23. *Keter Shem Tov*, 28. For a more complete explanation of this process, see *Transforming Darkness into Light*.

24. For a full explanation of these 15 contact points and their various Kabbalistic applications, see *Body, Mind, and Soul*, pp. 231-4.

PART II

DIVINE EMANATIONS

And God said: "Let us make man in our image after our likeness and let them rule over the fish of the sea and the birds of the sky and over the cattle and over all of the earth, and over every creeping thing that creeps on the earth." And God created man in His own image, in the image of God He created him; male and female He created them.

Genesis 1:26-27

Models: Keys to the Mind 4

BEFORE DELVING INTO MYSTICAL PRINCIPLES AND CONCEPTS, IT IS necessary to understand the significance attached in Kabbalah to the formulation of models and their use in creating correspondences between various facets of reality. Kabbalah uses models and correspondences in order to excite our minds and hearts, unlocking hidden talents and emotions and correcting our negative habits.

Correspondence

In the later books of the Bible, the word "kabbalah" is used in the sense of acceptance, or receptivity. Hence, since the Middle Ages, it has been used to describe the hidden tradition carefully received (and then transmitted) from generation to generation. However, in the Five Books of Moses,[1] the essential source of meaning for every Hebrew word, "kabbalah" means correspondence. How did the grammatical root of "correspondence" come to denote the act of receiving? The answer to this question points us to what is perhaps the deepest reason that so many people are today drawn to Kabbalah: our longing to be like God.

God's purpose, as stated explicitly in the book of Psalms, was that mankind embody, that is receive, His essence: "I [God] said 'you [mankind] are *Elokim*.'"[2] God created mankind with the yearning that He be able to transfer His benevolent essence to us. The Primordial Serpent built his case for enticing Eve into eating from the forbidden fruit of the Tree of Knowledge (of Good and Evil) on the allure of embodying God's essence. It claimed that by eating from the Tree of Knowledge, "you [mankind] shall become like *Elokim*, conscious of good and evil."[3] Because Adam and Eve ate from the forbidden fruit of the Tree of Knowledge, their knowledge/consciousness did indeed alter to include moral categories like good and evil, but in the process they also lost the higher consciousness upon which the transfer and embodiment of God's essence was dependent. As a result they were banished from the Garden of Eden.

Twenty-six generations later (26 is also the numerical value of God's essential Name, *Havayah*), the children of Abraham, Isaac, and Jacob, led by Moses out of their bondage in Egypt, merited to receive the consciousness-altering and refining Torah at Mt. Sinai. The Torah states explicitly (in the third to last of its 613 commandments) that we are commanded to emulate the Almighty. The simple meaning of this cherished goal of life is that we adopt the Almighty's attributes of loving-kindness, patience, charity, etc. Achieving this requires that we share God's thought and His perspective on reality, though naturally there has been debate between the sages of the Torah as to what extent this is possible. Indeed, by studying the Torah, both in its revealed and concealed aspects, we come to align, or calibrate our consciousness such that it matches that of the Almighty. By doing so, we are able to receive and reveal our particular portion of the Divine in a positive and constructive manner.[4]

Clearly, the Almighty's Infinite nature makes it impossible for a finite and limited human being to emulate Him completely. Rational and philosophical thought would therefore leave our consciousness forever separate and severed from that of our Creator's, making any similarity impossible. Nonetheless, we cannot completely ignore the fact that God's original purpose in creating human beings *was* that we indeed be like Him. And this—God's statement of purpose—continually gnaws at these would-be bonds that the non-mystical conception of reality would like to place on our minds and hearts.

With the hurdles imposed by rationality set aside for the moment, let us ask: How can our minds be shaped such that they become a worthy vessel to reveal God's essence? How can our limited being become a vessel for embodying the Divine essence? The answer lies in this special way of thinking about, organizing, and understanding our world, known as thinking in correspondences, the core of the Kabbalistic methodology.

God's Signature

Kabbalah seeks to reveal our deepest essence, unite it with the Divine, and thus unlock our deepest potential as human beings. To do so we must be adept at using the infinite wisdom of the Torah's inner dimension to find God's signature, as it were, in every aspect of ourselves and the world around us. The Talmud explains that the Almighty is like a painter who signs his name on every work he completes; God has signed His Name on every facet of the universe, regardless of how big or how small.

Like a traditionally minded painter, sometimes the signature used by the Almighty turns out to actually be one of His holy Names, thereby making them a root-model for many Kabbalistic correspondences. Still, many other correspondences not directly based on God's Names are used in Kabbalah. Some of these will be covered in this book.

To uncover God's signature, Kabbalah uses models that form the basis for setting up correspondences. A correspondence may be made between the parts of the human body and the letters of God's Name; between the ten plagues in Egypt and the ten *sefirot*, and so forth.

Though using correspondences to calibrate the mind was used from the very first stages of the revelation of Kabbalah, it was the Arizal who made it into the cornerstone of the Kabbalistic methodology. In fact, correspondences are so integral to the study of Kabbalah, that it is impossible to engage in its study at even the most basic level without learning about them, their formulation, and their use.

A correspondence in Kabbalah can be as simple as the interpretation of a symbol (this would be a one dimensional correspondence; we will give examples of such symbolism as the chapter proceeds). But more often than not a correspondence is multifaceted and is presented as a model that contains many elements. Every correspondence seeks to both order and translate (or map) elements from one frame of reference to another.

As a first example let us offer one of the simplest models introduced in a less esoteric text, the Talmud. The sages explain that the soul, as it resides in the body has five different properties,[5] which correspond to the five properties of the Almighty as He dwells in the world.[6] The sages learnt this correspondence from the fact that in chapters 103 and 104 of Psalms, the phrase "May my soul praise God" is repeated five times. That the soul can praise God seems to imply that there is some similarity between them. The five parts of the correspondence are as follows (in the order in which they appear in the Talmud):

the soul	God
fills the entire body	fills the entire world
sees but cannot be seen	sees but cannot be seen
nourishes the entire body	nourishes the entire world
is pure	is pure
sits in an inner chamber	sits in an inner chamber

The meaning and significance of each of these properties is worthy of elaboration, which we will defer for the present. For the moment let us concentrate on the underlying structure of this correspondence. First we note that it has five parts.

Elsewhere, based on the same observation—that the phrase "May my soul praise God" appears five times in chapters 103 and 104 of Psalms—the sages teach that the soul has five names, which are:

• the singular one (*yechidah*)
• the living one (*chayah*)

- soul (*neshamah*)
- spirit (*ru'ach*)
- anima (*nefesh*)

Amazingly, though not stated explicitly in any Kabbalistic text, the sum of the numerical values of all five names of the soul, in Hebrew, is exactly equal to the numerical value of the phrase which is repeated five times, "May my soul praise God"!

נֶפֶשׁ רוּחַ נְשָׁמָה חַיָּה יְחִידָה = בָּרְכִי נַפְשִׁי אֶת יְ׳׳הוה = 1099

Since the soul has five properties *and* five names it is obvious that there is a one-to-one correspondence between them. In this case, knowing which name corresponds to which property is the fruit of laborious study over the various meanings and connotations of the names themselves. To aid the construction of the model it is necessary to first correlate each set of five components with the most basic Kabbalistic model that has five components: the essential Name of the Almighty, *Havayah*.

Though *Havayah* has only four letters (*yud*, *hei*, *vav*, *hei*), Kabbalah explains that a certain calligraphic mark on the first letter, the *yud*, called the tip of the *yud* (*kutzo shel yud*) represents a fifth, concealed component, while each of the four explicit letters of the Name represent four revealed components. These five components of God's essential Name, *Havayah*, form a basic template to which every five-tiered model can be applied, including our own two examples: the names of the soul and its properties. Both correspond to the five components of God's essential Name. But how do they correspond? Which property corresponds to which letter of the Name *Havayah*?

To correctly correspond two similarly structured models is the heart of the art of contemplative Kabbalah, and requires years of study and an inner sense for parallels, described in the Talmud as the ability to find the similar in two things (*ledamot milta le'milta*)[7]. But once the model has been constructed correctly, it becomes spiritually alive and can provide a basis for deep contemplation and meditation on its subject.

In all, the final correspondence of all three sets of 5-components follows the order of the properties of the soul as listed in the Talmud (beginning with the correspondence to the lowest level of the soul, the anima):

letter of *Havayah*	name of the soul	property of the soul
tip of *yud*	the singular one	dwells in an inner chamber
yud	the living one	is pure
hei	soul	nourishes the body
vav	spirit	sees and is not seen
hei	anima	fills the body

Once the components of a correspondence have been ordered, according to a Kabbalistic model, the correspondence becomes an invitation to understand, explore, and innovate.[8]

Perhaps the best way to understand the role of the model is to liken it to a key. This key is not for a physical lock but for opening still secured areas of the mind. Because of the nature of the mind, Kabbalistic models are always holographic, a more advanced topic that we will not cover in this introductory text. Once a Kabbalistic model is inserted into the mind, it acts as like a key that has been inserted into a lock—a new door is opened. The mind opens and becomes aware of a new way to see the world and its inner structure. People, events, and places that had previously seemed dissociated and confusing, suddenly yield new levels of connection and meaning.

Kabbalistic Models and the Imagination

Thus, Kabbalah is always interested in understanding God's relationship and perspective on creation and is concerned with explaining various correspondences and parallelisms implicit within existence. In so doing, Kabbalistic discourse develops, molds, and deepens our powers of association, which are responsible for envisioning that which the physical eye cannot see.

By molding our powers of imagination and association, Kabbalah serves a central role in rectifying it.[9] An unchecked imagination tends to invite fantasies that are aimed at gratifying the baser drives, but the study of Kabbalah employs it in the service of the spiritual instincts, using it to imagine an array of harmonious connections within reality, as well as connections between God and His creation.

The Origin of the Kabbalistic Templates

We are now better prepared to appreciate the methodology of the master Kabbalists who formulated their insights in the form of correspondences and by inserting these models into their minds, developed their relationship with God bringing His essence further into their lives.

As mentioned above, the templates employed in Kabbalah are rooted in its very origins, even though it was the Arizal who brought their use to full fruition. The first sentence of the first Kabbalistic work, *Sefer Yetzirah*, describes the three most basic templates, comprising 4, 10, and 22 parts, respectively:

> With thirty-two wondrous pathways of wisdom, God (*Havayah*) engraved…. He created His world with three books: a scribe, a book, and a story.

God's essential Name, *Havayah*, comprises *four* letters and is the first template. The "thirty-two wondrous pathways of wisdom" divide into the *ten sefirot* (the emanations of Divine light and energy, which will be reviewed in chapters 6 and 7) and the *twenty-two* letters of the Hebrew *alephbet*.[10] Together they are the building blocks with which the Creator, *Havayah*, created (and continually recreates) the world. Thus, we have in this opening sentence a description of the three most basic templates used in Kabbalah:

- ◆ to analyze and order something that has four levels or components, the classic frame of reference in Kabbalah is the essential four-letter Name of God, *Havayah* (as we saw in our example above, the Name *Havayah* also serves as the template for a five component model).

♦ to analyze and order a subject that has ten components, Kabbalah uses the template of the ten *sefirot*.

♦ for a subject with twenty-two components, the template of choice is the twenty-two letters of the Hebrew *alephbet*.

The second part of this opening sentence describes these three templates using more symbolic (and literary) language. The three primordial books of creation it refers to, "a scribe," "a book," and "a story" correspond to these same template-models (of four, of ten and of twenty-two components). The "scribe" is the Almighty Himself, who is the author of the "book" of creation, and whose four letter essential Name is sealed at its every level. The "book" is creation itself, which is inherently modeled using the ten *sefirot*, which in turn can be revealed to be inscribed on every page of the book of creation—i.e., the Torah. The "story" told in the book of creation is related using the twenty-two letters of the Hebrew *alephbet*, making Hebrew the ideal language for describing our reality, spiritual as well as physical, natural, along with human.

In the following chapters we will take a deeper look at these three most fundamental models, or templates. We will begin our examination with the twenty-two Hebrew letters, then turn to the ten *sefirot*, and finally (in Part III of this book) to the four letters of God's essential Name, *Havayah* (as well as His other Names and connotations, all of which derive ultimately from His four-letter Name).

Notes:

1. Exodus 26:5, "*The corresponding loops shall be [like] a woman toward her sister.*" These "corresponding loops," when clasped together, joined the two sections of the covering draped over the Tabernacle that, in the Holy of Holies, housed the Ark of the Covenant.
2. Psalms 82:6.
3. Genesis 3:5.

4. The Hebrew word דַּעַת can be translated in three ways: knowledge, consciousness, and perspective. Thus the Tree of Knowledge is also the Tree of Consciousness and the Tree of Perspective. Knowledge, consciousness, and perspective denote three steps in the fulfillment of the commandment to be like God.

    Knowledge refers to the objectivity that today is most prevalent in science and serves to free us from false beliefs and primitive fears, both examples of idol worship. Knowledge thus serves to elevate our conception of our surroundings, in turn permitting us to elevate them.

    Consciousness refers to the subjective recognition of our own souls. Whereas it can be the basis of an egotistic attitude, when used incorrectly, the humanity revealed by subjectivity is what allows us to connect with other souls.

    Perspective refers to the Almighty's perspective on reality. What He sees is not what we see. Of Moses the Torah says: "And he saw God's picture" (Numbers 12:8), which in Chassidut is explained to mean that Moses was able to see our reality from God's own perspective. This is the highest state of resembling the Almighty that a human being can reach.

5. See also *The Mystery of Marriage*, pp. 14-19.

6. *Berachot* 10a.

7. *Ibid.* 19a, *Yevamot* 109b. On the difficulty of corresponding things correctly, see *Shulchan Aruch Yoreh Dei'ah* 124:19. On the role of correspondence see the Alter Rebbe's *Likutei Torah, Shir Hashirim* 42d.

8. This correspondence was explained in the Hebrew volume *Esa Einai*, pp. 120-7. The advanced reader is referred there.

9. See *The Mystery of Marriage*, ch. 2.

10. 4, 10, and 22 form a quadratic series whose base is 6:

$$4 \qquad 10 \qquad 22$$

$$6 \qquad 12$$

$$6$$

Finding the numbers preceding 4, we see that the series mirrors itself,

22	10	4	4	10	22
-12	-6	0	6	12	
6	6	6	6		

implying that the 4 letters of God's essential Name, the 10 *sefirot*, and the 22 letters of the Hebrew alphabet mirror the congruent but hidden aspects of reality.

Letters: Building Blocks of the Universe

5

KABBALAH, EVEN AT THE MOST INTRODUCTORY LEVEL, REQUIRES familiarity with the Hebrew alphabet. To study Kabbalah in depth one must also be able to read and understand basic texts like the Bible and the Mishnah. Though Hebrew was not a spoken language for almost fifteen-hundred years, during that time scholars of the Torah, including Kabbalists, wrote some of the most magnificent Hebrew texts in existence. Consequently, to study the Torah in general and Kabbalah in particular, speaking Hebrew is not as necessary as being able to correctly read and understand it. As befitting an introductory text, we have kept our instruction of Hebrew to a minimum, and have tried to stress those aspects of the language that reveal its mystical and creative power.

The Hebrew Alphabet

The Hebrew Alphabet[1]—called the *alef-beit*, after its first two letters—comprises twenty-two letters. These letters are all consonants. Vowels are generally indicated with diacritical marks above, beneath, or after letters; however, four of the twenty-two consonants (א, ה, ו, י) are used to indicate vowel-sounds as well.

Each letter possesses a numerical value, which is very significant in understanding the hidden meaning of each word. Indeed, Hebrew words and phrases can be compared based on their numerical values. This technique is called *gematria*, and is one of the cornerstones of Kabbalistic analysis and thought.

Sefer Yetzirah explains that the twenty-two Hebrew letters are the basic energy building blocks of creation whose combinations and permutations represent all the creative forces that God used when He, as it were, spoke creation into being. Kabbalah teaches that words formed by combinations and permutations of letters are the vessels through which the creative process continues to take place.

Hebrew (unlike Roman languages like English) is logically structured. It begins with 22 letters that act as the building blocks. These 22 letters then join to form 231 *sha'arim* (gates). Finally, three letter *shorashim* (roots), are formed from the gates. Every single word in Hebrew is based on a letter, gate or root, with the predominant majority being directly based on a root. Thus to truly understand the underlying logic and meaning of a word in Hebrew, it is necessary to reconstruct its root.

Sefer Yetzirah also divides the twenty-two Hebrew letters into the following three groups based on both grammatical and spiritual considerations:

* three *mother* letters
* seven *double* letters
* twelve *simple* letters

The various letters are further identified with corresponding elements (such as fire and water), with corresponding gifts (such as wisdom and wealth), with corresponding senses (such as hearing and sight), as well as with corresponding body parts.

The three *mother* letters—*alef, mem,* and *shin*—correspond to the three primal elements of creation—air, water, and fire respectively, and to the three general divisions of the body: chest corresponds to air; abdomen to water; and head to fire.

letter		element	part of body
alef	א	air	chest
mem	מ	water	abdomen
shin	ש	fire	head

The seven *double* letters—*beit, gimel, dalet, kaf, pei, reish, tav*—correspond in the body to the seven *gateways* of the head. Each one serves as a gateway for one of the senses of sight, hearing, smell, and taste—the sensations of external reality—allowing them to enter the consciousness of the psyche. Each gateway, when sanctified, also serves as a portal through which to receive a Divine gift or blessing as follows:

letter		gift	gateway
bet	ב	wisdom	right eye
gimel	ג	wealth	right ear
dalet	ד	children	right nostril
kaf	כ	life	left eye
pei	פ	sovereignty	left ear
reish	ר	peace	left nostril
tav	ת	grace	mouth

The twelve *simple* letters—*hei, vav, zayin, chet, tet, yud, lamed, nun, samech, ayin, tzadik, kuf*—correspond to twelve limbs and organs of the body. Each controls (often in a most mysterious way, for no overt relationship is apparent) a spiritual faculty of the soul (also the particularized talent of each of the twelve tribes of Israel):

letter		faculty	limb/organ
hei	ה	speech, expression	right leg
vav	ו	thought	right kidney
zayin	ז	walking, progress	left leg
chet	ח	sight, perception	right hand
tet	ט	hearing, comprehension	left kidney
yud	י	action, rectification	left hand
lamed	ל	touch, sexuality	gall bladder
nun	נ	smell, sensitivity	intestines
samech	ס	sleep, dreaming	lower bowels
ayin	ע	anger, indignation	liver
tzadik	צ	eating, taste	stomach
kuf	ק	laughter, exuberance	spleen

Gematria: The Numerical Value of the Hebrew Letters

As noted above, each of the twenty-two letters of the Hebrew alphabet has a numerical value, making it possible for Hebrew letters and words to be translated into numbers. This technique is called *gematria*. There are several systems of *gematria*, and it would take a book in itself to explain them all. The system generally used is the *absolute value* or the *normative value* system. In this system, the letters are assigned numerical values in order as follows:

alef	א	1	*yud*	י	10	*kuf*	ק	100
bet	ב	2	*kaf*	כ	20	*reish*	ר	200
gimel	ג	3	*lamed*	ל	30	*shin*	ש	300
dalet	ד	4	*mem*	מ	40	*tav*	ת	400
hei	ה	5	*nun*	נ	50	*final kaf*	ך	500
vav	ו	6	*samech*	ס	60	*final mem*	ם	600
zayin	ז	7	*ayin*	ע	70	*final nun*	ן	700
chet	ח	8	*pei*	פ	80	*final pei*	ף	800
tet	ט	9	*tzadik*	צ	90	*final tzadik*	ץ	900

In Kabbalah, the calculation of the numerical equivalence of letters, words, or phrases, helps us gain insight into relationships between different concepts, words, and ideas. The assumption behind *gematria* is that numerical equivalence is not coincidental. Since the world was created through God's "speech," each letter represents a different creative force. Thus, the numerical equivalence of two words reveals an internal connection between the creative potentials of each one.[2]

In order to get a taste of how this discipline is used in the study of Kabbalah, we will present a few examples, each one applying the wisdom of *gematria* to reveal a truth in a unique way.

The first example we saw above: The numerical value of the Hebrew word *Kabbalah*, which is written in Hebrew קַבָּלָה, is 137. 137 is also the combined value of the Hebrew words for "wisdom," written חָכְמָה and equal to 73, and "prophecy," written נְבוּאָה and equal to 64, as noted above. It follows therefore that Kabbalah includes both powers of wisdom and prophecy. As it turns out, and as discussed in length above, Kabbalah actually is the offspring of these two traditions in the study of the Torah.

At times, words or phrases that are equal in their numerical value seem to clash in meaning. For example, the numerical value of the Hebrew word for "humility," spelled שֵׁפֶל is 410, as is the numerical value of the word for "arrogance," written גֵּאוּת. In Hebrew, these words also mean "low tide" and "high tide," respectively, as clear a pair of opposites as can be found. In such cases, the two words either rectify or complement one another. Thus, humility is the sentiment (and faculty, as will be seen later) that can rectify one's arrogance and feelings of self-centeredness. Likewise, "low tide" is the complement—the other side of the coin—of "high tide." Incidentally, many people have come to think of *gematria* as mere sophistry because they mistakenly believe that anything can be shown to be equal to anything. There are indeed some *gematria* analyses that are less informative than others, but on the whole they all carry some meaning. The more surprising the *gematria* the more information content it carries.

One such surprising *gematria* is that the Hebrew word for Messiah, מָשִׁיחַ (358), is equal to the Hebrew word for the Primordial Serpent, נָחָשׁ. Kabbalah and Chassidut explain this numerical equality in length, the short of the matter being that it is only the Messiah himself who will be able to do final battle with the Primordial Serpent (the symbol of our evil inclination), conquer it, kill its external manifestation while simultaneously domesticating it and placing its inner essence under his control.

Many gematrias need to be analyzed symbolically. Except for the Five Books of Moses, because of the nature of prophecy, most of the Bible uses symbolic language. Because of this, and because of the need to relate amorphous and non-corporeal ideas, most of the exegetic tradition in Judaism is rich in symbolic language. For instance, when discussing the topic of love, Chassidic discourses, calling upon various Biblical sources, note that there are different types of love. There is love that is likened to water, love that is likened to fire, and love that is likened to pleasure. Water, fire, and pleasure are obviously symbolic and are meant to describe in a more palpable way the nature of different states of love.

Chassidut explains that natural love—a natural sense of affinity and attraction between two souls or between man and God—is likened to water. This is the love of brother to sister, always present in the heart and requiring no more than a thought of one another to arouse and bring into consciousness. On the other hand, love of God that is likened to fire, as the love between spouses, is aroused by meditation—especially meditation upon the unity and singularity of the Creator. Every Jew is commanded to meditate upon God's unity at least twice daily by reciting the first verse of the passage in Deuteronomy known (for its first word) as the *Shema*: "Hear, O Israel: *God* is our God, *God* is one."[3] The next verse states that from this meditation is born love for God: "And you shall love *God* your God with all your heart, with all your soul, and with all your might." Now to our *gematria*: the numerical value of the Hebrew word for a flame (particularly the glowing flame in a red-hot coal), which can be used to light a fire, שַׁלְהֶבֶת, is 737. This is also the numerical value of the Hebrew phrase describing the love that the *Shema* meditation enheartens: "with all your heart, and with all your soul, and with all your might," בְּכָל לְבָבְךָ וּבְכָל נַפְשְׁךָ וּבְכָל מְאֹדֶךָ! This *gematria* reveals the functional underpinnings of a very complex process in the human experience: meditation acts as a flame and kindles love that is likened to fire. But what exactly is love that is likened to fire? From this *gematria* we learn that it is the love described as loving God with all your heart, soul, and might. Of course, there is still much to be understood in the way of defining what "heart, soul, and might" are, but this *gematria* provides a primary working definition that can lead to a deeper understanding of what meditation can arouse in our lives.

To add a little cherry on top, note that the numerical value of the Hebrew word used to describe God's unity and singularity, "one," אֶחָד, is 13, exactly the value of the word for "love," אַהֲבָה, indicating a contextual relationship between the subject of the meditation (God's unity) and its outcome: love.[4]

God and Nature

One of the most frequently cited gematrias has to do with a Hebrew word that did not even exist until the Middle Ages: *hateva*, הַטֶּבַע, which means "nature." There is no word for "nature" in Biblical, nor Rabbinic Hebrew. The word used today was first coined somewhere in the middle part of the Medieval age. Its etymology is apparently related to the verb meaning "to stamp" (לְהַטְבִּיעַ),[5] which is used in the sense of stamping a coin with an image. We mention this because it is a beautiful example of how Judaism understands that the natural world is stamped, figuratively, with the signature of the Almighty.

We have noted that God has many Names in Hebrew (which we will discuss in full in Part III of this book). Nature, הַטֶּבַע, possesses the identical numerical value, 86, as does one of the Names of God, *Elokim*, אֱ־לֹהִים, implying that this Name of God is most closely associated with nature. This equivalence is especially significant because *Elokim* is the Name used to describe God as the Creator in the first chapter of Genesis. Furthermore, *Elokim* appears exactly 32 times in the story of the six days of creation, alluding to the 32 Pathways of Wisdom, with which *Sefer Yetzirah* says that God created the world.

The Lunar Cycle and the Human Body

Another fascinating example of how *gematria* works comes from the Book of Ecclesiastes.[6] In a well-known passage from it, King Solomon states that there is a time for everything:

> A *time* to be born, and a *time* to die; a *time* to plant, and a *time* to pluck up that which is planted.
> A *time* to kill, and a *time* to heal; a *time* to break down, and a *time* to build up.
> A *time* to weep, and a *time* to laugh; a *time* to mourn, and a *time* to dance.

A *time* to cast away stones, and a *time* to gather stones
together; a *time* to embrace, and a *time* to refrain from
embracing.
A *time* to seek, and a *time* to lose; a *time* to keep, and a *time* to
cast away.
A *time* to rend, and a *time* to sew; a *time* to keep silent, and a
time to speak.
A *time* to love, and a *time* to hate; a *time* of war, and a *time* of
peace.

In all, there are 28 instances of one of the Hebrew words for time,
עֵת, which divide into 14 pairs, one positive time in contrast with
its negative conterpart. The number 28 is intrinsically associated
with a lunar month, which is made up of four 7-day lunar quarters
totaling 28 days. The waxing and the waning of the moon thus
represent the full cycle of terrestrial time. These 28 times are also
alluded to in the verse, "In Your hand are my times."[7] But, the
allusion is not just the use of the same word, "time" in Ecclesiastes
and "times" in this verse (an analytic method known in Rabbinic
methodology as *gezeirah shavah*). Rather, we can use *gematria* to
illustrate a beautiful example of self-reference—a textual
phenomenon in which something relates back to itself.

If the first letter of the word בְּיָדְךָ, which serves as the prefix
letter *bet*, בּ, meaning "in," is understood as a *gematria* (בּ = 2), then
the revised meaning of the word would be "Your two hands."
Continuing this thread of thought and taking the Hebrew word for
"hand," יָד, we see that its numerical value is 14.[8] Since there are
two hands, then we are speaking of 2 · 14 = 28, referring to the 28
times, which are, symbolically, always in the hands of God. As
noted above, the 28 times divide into 14 positive times, symbolized
by the right hand, and 14 negative times, symbolized by the left
hand. So in this particular example of *gematria*, we have analyzed
each part of a word separately, and based on this analysis
reconstructed an alternate, albeit revealing commentary on a
particular verse.[9]

Now, let us take the ideas just introduced another step further and continue to develop them with the help of *gematria*. According to the sages, each hand possesses 30 *eivarim*, usually translated as "limbs," but actually referring to sections of human bone and flesh that would cause ritual impurity when dead.[10] Together, the two hands possess 60 such parts, which themselves allude to the secret of the 60 letters that make up the Priestly Blessing in its original Hebrew:[11]

יְבָרֶכְךָ יהוה וְיִשְׁמְרֶךָ.

יָאֵר יהוה פָּנָיו אֵלֶיךָ וִיחֻנֶּךָּ.

יִשָּׂא יהוה פָּנָיו אֵלֶיךָ וְיָשֵׂם לְךָ שָׁלוֹם.

The equality between the number of letters in the Priestly Blessing and the number of parts in the hands offers one explanation for why the priests raise their hands when reciting this blessing in front of the congregation. The light of each of the sixty letters emanates from one of the 60 parts of the priest's hands.

Because each hand has 30 parts, each is represented by the Hebrew letter *lamed*, whose numerical value is 30. The great medieval Kabbalist, Rabbi Abraham Abulafia showed that when two letters *lamed* are drawn so as to face one another they form the physical shape of the heart. Indeed, this same idea is alluded to in the word "heart" in Hebrew, which is spelled לֵב: a *lamed* followed by a *bet*—which as we saw above is equal to 2—implying that a "heart" is actually 2 letters *lamed*. From this we learn that spiritual energy and blessing flows from the heart to the two hands and from the hands, in the Priestly Blessing, to the people of Israel.[12]

Returning to the numerical value of the word "hand" in Hebrew, which is 14, we note that in the Five Books of Moses, the grammatical root of "healing," רפא, appears exactly 14 times ("hand" in Hebrew can also mean power, or ability). These 14 instances of healing imply a spiritual connection between healing and the (power of the) hand, suggesting that there is healing power in the physician's hand.

Another important *gematria* related to healing: According to Kabbalah, disease and pain derive from a state of spiritual deficiency or emptiness. In Kabbalah, the state of spiritual wholeness is associated with the number 50.[13] Indeed, the numerical value of the Hebrew word for someone who is sick, חוֹלֶה, is 49, one less than 50, indicating that a sick person is lacking in the spiritual wholeness necessary for good health. By corollary, healing is the act of filling or completing the patient's spiritual state of being.

We have offered a small sampling of how *gematria* is used in Kabbalah. Throughout our other volumes you may find many others, as well. One small remaining caveat is that we have only been using zero-dimensional *gematria*, that is, where each letter is simply replaced by a number. To fully appreciate the power of *gematria*, it is necessary to present numbers in multi-dimensional geometric or figurate forms. But, that is a topic for a forthcoming volume.

Notes:

1. See *The Hebrew Letters: Channels of Creative Consciousness* for an in-depth introduction to the letters of the Hebrew alphabet.
2. *Tanya, Sha'ar HaYichud VeHaEmunah*, chapters 1 and 12.
3. Deuteronomy 6:4. "God," in the translation of this verse refers to the Name *Elokim*.
4. When the values of these two words, "one" and "love," in Hebrew are added together (both equal 13) we get 26, the *gematria* (numerical value) of God's essential Name, *Havayah*, as explained.
5. This word also means "to drown."
6. Ecclesiastes 3:2-8.
7. Psalms 31:16.
8. Incidentally, there are exactly 14 revealed phalanges (bones of the digits) in each hand, beautifully relating the Hebrew word for "hand" with the hand itself.
9. For another example of this type of mixed analysis see *The Art of Education*, p. 119.

10. *Mishnah Ohalot* 1:8. There are a total of 248 such body parts, or limbs, which is also the number of positive commandments in the Five Books of Moses.

11. Numbers 6:24-26, which translated means:

    May God bless you and protect you;

    May God shine His countenance upon you and be gracious to you;

    May God turn His countenance toward you and grant you peace."

12. See our website for mystical Jewelry based on Rabbi Abulafia's teaching: www.inner.org/jewelry.

13. The original term is 50 Gates of Purity, which correspond to the 50 Gates of Understanding and are related to the 32 Paths of Wisdom. For more on understanding and wisdom, see chapter 7.

Sefirot: Divine Energy   6

PROBABLY THE BEST-KNOWN HEBREW WORD THAT KABBALAH IS responsible for introducing to non-Hebrew speakers is *sefirah* (not to be confused with the English "sphere") and its plural form, *sefirot*. This is because the most fundamental model used in Kabbalah is that of the ten *sefirot*. Like many other words used in Kabbalah, the most practical approach for getting a sense of what it refers to is by looking at its various meanings in Biblical Hebrew.

In Hebrew, the meanings of a word can be studied only by first finding the word's grammatical root and then looking at all the different usages, the different nouns or verbs that the root is used in. The three-letter root of the word *sefirah*—*samech-pei-reish*—bears three distinct meanings that are relevant to the word itself:

First, this root is used in the sense of an emanation of Divine light. *Sefirah* is derived from the Biblical *sapir*, meaning sapphire, whose brilliance is associated with the heavenly throne envisioned by the prophets.[1]

The word s*efirah* also denotes a specific attribute or trait through which God expresses Himself in the world. In this sense God is like an author of a book that expresses himself through the narrative he writes. The Hebrew words for "story" (*sippur*) and "book" (*sefer*) are from the root of *sefirah*.

Finally, the Hebrew word for "number" (*mispar*) derives from the root of *sefirah*, alluding to the abstract underlying mathematical structure of creation.

Because of its varied meanings, special attention must be paid to the word *sefirah*. Even though in Kabbalah it always designates a Divine emanation, nonetheless, its meaning fluctuates with the context in which it is being used. In general, the three major contextual usages of the ten *sefirot* are (1) the ten manifestations of God; (2) the ten powers or faculties of the soul; or, (3) the ten structural forces of nature. In Chassidic terminology, these three contexts are considered the three basic dimensions of reality. In the terminology of Chassidut they are called: Divinity, Souls, and Worlds.[2]

When speaking of the manner in which God's self-expression is perceived, the ten *sefirot* are understood as ten manifestations of Divinity. We find this phenomenon reflected in the four-letters of the essential Name of God, *Havayah*, each of which corresponds to a *sefirah*, or group of *sefirot*, as will be explained later. When reflecting on how Divinity is projected into the living experience of a human being, the *sefirot* become manifest as the ten powers of the soul. Finally, we find that the *sefirot* are also cast as the basic structural forces orchestrated in forming our external reality, for example the components of our bodies. In this chapter, we will examine the meaning of each of the ten *sefirot* within all three contexts.

Note that though we usually speak of ten *sefirot*, we will be discussing a model with eleven *sefirot*. This is because two of the *sefirot*, crown and knowledge, are two dimensions of a single force, as will become clearer as we progress.

The Model of the *Sefirot*

In Kabbalistic texts (especially those following the revelation of the teachings of the Arizal), the *sefirot* are configured, and graphically depicted, as lying along three parallel vertical axes, like so:

כֶּתֶר
keter
crown

בִּינָה
binah
understanding

חָכְמָה
chochmah
wisdom

דַּעַת
da'at
knowledge

גְּבוּרָה
gevurah
might

חֶסֶד
chesed
loving-kindness

תִּפְאֶרֶת
tiferet
beauty

הוֹד
hod
acknowledgment

נֶצַח
netzach
victory

יְסוֹד
yesod
foundation

מַלְכוּת
malchut
kingdom

Each axis represents a mode of Divine influence within creation. In the idiom of the *Tikunei Zohar*, one of the earlier Kabbalistic texts, the axes are described as "one is long, one is short, and one is intermediate." The left axis is relatively short compared to the right axis, while the middle axis acts as a harmonizing and balancing force between them, hence its description as an intermediate. The adjectives "short" and "long" associated with the left and right axes provide a visual metaphor for the delimiting (shortening, as it were) powers inherent in the *sefirot* lying along the left axis as opposed to the expansive (lengthening) powers of the *sefirot* lying along the right axis. In more anthropomorphic language, the "long" right axis exhibits the attributes of patience and forgiveness, while the "short" left axis tends to alacrity and forceful judgment, with the middle axis providing a balanced inter-inclusion of the two.

This visual configuration of the *sefirot* is variously referred to in Kabbalistic literature as a "ladder,"[3] a "tree,"[4] or as the supernal "image" of God. According to this last designation, the configuration of the *sefirot* suggests both the physical image and the psychological/spiritual makeup of the human being, as they were fashioned in the image of God: "And God said: Let us make man in our image, after our likeness."[5] Thus, based on its position in this configuration, each *sefirah* is associated with a corresponding limb or organ in the human anatomy.[6]

The interaction between the various *sefirot* is depicted through a network of connecting channels that parallel the flow of Divine energy within creation. Their interactions suggest a division of the *sefirot* into three basic sub-groupings, each sub-group reflecting a common dynamic among the *sefirot* included therein. The three sub-groupings are:

- intellectual, or cognitive: wisdom, understanding, and knowledge
- emotive: loving-kindness, might, and beauty
- behavioral, or active: victory, acknowledgment, and foundation

This accounts for only 9 of the 11 *sefirot* appearing in the diagram. The first *sefirah*, crown, represents the super-intellectual (that which is beyond reason and common sense, normally represented by faith), and in a certain sense can be viewed as superimposed on this diagram from a different plane. The last *sefirah*, kingdom, can be viewed as either an appendage of the last sub-grouping, or as an independent entity receiving all the energies that precede it.

Sefirot and Divinity: The Story of Creation

Though the word *sefirah* should definitely be understood as carrying all three of the meanings noted above, when explaining the role of the *sefirot* as they pertain to the creative process, we stress the second meaning which links it with the idea of writing or narrative.

The Torah narrative of creation can be found in the first two chapters of the book of Genesis. However, in Kabbalistic and Chassidic writings the act of creation is not considered a one-time occurrence. Instead, because creation is meant to reveal the Almighty, it is actually an ongoing process, one that occurs at every instance and through which God is revealed to us anew (and differently) at every moment. Because creation is a recurring process, the role of the *sefirot* is even more essential, as every moment of time can be analyzed as based on the particular nature and functionality of the *sefirah* currently active.

It should be stated clearly from the outset that the Almighty, as He exists unto Himself, cannot be understood or even spoken about using any kind of human thought or language. Instead, man can meet God only through the prism of created reality. Through that prism, God appears to us in the form and manner that He chooses.[7]

The Torah describes the Almighty in terms of the 13 Divine attributes (also called the 13 Principles of Divine Mercy), with which God revealed Himself to Moses.[8] Kabbalah reveals that the 13 Divine attributes actually stem from the ten *sefirot*.[9]

The sages expound that the Almighty created the world with 10 utterances, or acts of Divine speech, that appear in Genesis.[10] Each of the 10 utterances is a unique manner in which God reveals Himself, for as already said, the basic prism through which He can be known is the act of creation.

In the context of creation, the *sefirot* represent the various stages of the process whereby God generated from within His own infinite being the progression of created realms that culminates in our finite physical universe. Outside of the creative process itself, but still within the context of Divinity, the *sefirot* function together as the components of a single metaphysical structure whose generative imprint can be identified at all levels, and within all aspects, of creation. Like the recurring motifs or themes in a novel, in this capacity, the model of the ten *sefirot* acts as a repeating structure in the universe, signing everything with the signature of the Almighty.

One last word about the *sefirot* in general: each of the ten *sefirot* comprises both a light and a vessel. Simply, the light of the *sefirah* is the Divine energy flowing within it; the vessel is the form or identity that the flow of energy takes in order to relate to some aspect of the world in a specific way. Inasmuch as all existence was created by means of the *sefirot*, they constitute the conceptual paradigm for understanding all reality. Divine energy itself appears in one of three forms known as: light, life-force, and, energy.[11]

Keter: the Crown

Crown, the first of the ten *sefirot*, corresponds to the super-conscious realm of experience. The image of a crown suggests that the faculties pertaining to this *sefirah* surround and envelope one's consciousness like an aura. That is why in Chassidut, the *sefirah* of crown is identified with our super-conscious realm. It is the spiritual counterpart of all of the soul's faculties and powers that are not directly observable or directly harnessable.

But, even as the crown is above and beyond all that is revealed and normal, it is also directly linked with the lowest, most mundane and most present of all the *sefirot*, kingdom; as the *Introduction to the Tikunei Zohar* states: "the supernal crown is the crown of kingdom."

The numerical value of this *sefirah*'s Hebrew name (כֶּתֶר) is 620. This is the full number of God's commandments to Israel: the 613 commandments of the Written Torah (the Five Books of Moses) together with the 7 commandments of the Oral Torah.[12]

The Hebrew text of the Ten Commandments[13] comprises 620 letters, hinting that all 620 commandments of the Torah are included within them.[14] In Kabbalah, the 620 commandments are referred to as 620 pillars of light that project from the crown (the ceiling) to connect it with the *sefirah* of kingdom (the floor). In Chassidut it is explained that these pillars of light encompass the souls of Israel that devotedly fulfill the will of the King of kings.

Chochmah: Wisdom

Wisdom, the second of the ten *sefirot*, is the first cognitive power of conscious intellect and is the primary force of creation by the Almighty.

Wisdom implies the ability to look deeply at some aspect of reality and ponder its essence until one succeeds in uncovering its axiomatic truth. These seeds of truth can then be conveyed to wisdom's companion power understanding for the sake of intellectual analysis and development.

Wisdom is the primary force in the creative process, as the Psalms declare: "You [God] have made them all with wisdom."[15] The first word of the Torah,[16] *bereisheet*, which is usually translated as "In the beginning [God created the heavens and the earth]," is translated by the *Targum Yerushalmi*, a Mishnaic era translation and commentary of the Torah in Aramaic, as: "With wisdom [God created the heavens and the earth]."

The full numerical value of the first verse of the Torah—"In the beginning God created the heavens and the earth"—is 2701, which is the sum of all numbers from 1 to 73 (denoted in arithmetic as the triangle of 73). 73 is the numerical value of wisdom (חָכְמָה).

Binah: Understanding

Understanding is the third of the ten *sefirot*, and the second conscious power of intellect in creation.

The name understanding implies the ability to examine the degree of truth or falsehood inherent in a particular idea. This power of analysis is associated in the Bible with the sense of hearing: "the ear examines words."[17] The most well known example of this association can be found in the quintessential tenet of Judaism: "Hear, O Israel: *God* is our God, *God* is One," [18] where the word hearing means understanding.

Another intellectual trait identified with the *sefirah* of understanding is the ability to clearly explain and elucidate concepts, both to oneself and to others and as such it is symbolized in Kabbalah as the wide river.[19]

The Hebrew word for understanding, *binah*, shares the same grammatical root as the word *bein*, which means "between." Thus understanding possesses the intellectual power to distinguish and differentiate *between* ideas or objects. Understanding is considered the second brain—sometimes described as lying *between* wisdom and knowledge.

In Kabbalah, wisdom and understanding are referred to as the father and the mother. Their union is called the higher union. The higher union is constant and therefore these two *sefirot* are referred to in the *Zohar* as "two companions that never separate."[20] The higher union is necessary for sustaining our reality, which is manifested through the continual re-creation of the world.

Numerically, the sum of wisdom (חָכְמָה = 73) and understanding (בִּינָה = 67) is 140, which is also the sum of all square numbers from 1 to 7 ($1 + 4 + 9 + 16 + 25 + 36 + 49 = 140$). This numerical equality reveals that the union of wisdom and understanding is indeed the spiritual source of the 7 days of creation, the 7 children. In the minds of the father and mother the children are present in their ultimate state of perfection (a square number represents a perfected state of being).

Da'at: Knowledge

The *sefirah* of knowledge is the third and last of the conscious powers of intellect in creation.[21]

Generally, knowledge is only enumerated among the *sefirot* when crown is not. This is because knowledge serves as a reflection of the inner dimension of the crown, which itself lies beyond the realm of consciousness. For this same reason, knowledge appears in the configuration of the *sefirot* along the middle axis, directly beneath crown.

Knowledge is associated with the powers of memory and concentration, powers that rely upon one's sensitivity to the potential meaningfulness of those ideas generated in consciousness through the powers of wisdom and understanding. This sensitivity is in its essence super-rational and derives from the connection that knowledge has to crown.

In the *Zohar*, knowledge is referred to as "the key that includes six."[22] Similar to the metaphor of a lock and key discussed above (in chapter 4), knowledge is the intellectual key to the six *chambers of the heart* (a symbolic name for the *sefirot* from loving-kindness to foundation) and fills them with life force. Each of these chambers, when filled with knowledge, is referred to as a particular *dei'ah*, meaning an attitude of the soul.

The numerical value of *dei'ah* (דֵּעָה) is 79. And, 79 · 6 = 474, the numerical value of *da'at* (דַּעַת).

Chesed: Loving-kindness

Loving-kindness is the fourth of the ten *sefirot*, and the first of the emotive attributes within creation.

Loving-kindness is represented by the first day of creation. On this day God created the goodly light, the light of loving-kindness for all. In the Torah, the first day of creation is called "one day" (*yom echad*), which can also mean "the day of one." On this day all of creation was embraced as one, in love, by the oneness of the Creator.[23]

Of the first day of creation it is said in Psalms, "By day, God will command His loving-kindness."[24] The Hebrew form of the noun for "day" in this verse, *yomam*, is neither singular (*yom*), nor plural (*yamim*), but rather a form not found elsewhere. As explained in the *Zohar*,[25] the unique form *yomam* illustrates that the first day of creation was different from the other days as it was "a day that accompanies all days."[26] As the first day of creation corresponds to the *sefirah* of loving-kindness, from this special trait of the first day, we learn that loving-kindness radiates its light to all the other six *sefirot*: from might to kingdom.

The numerical value of loving-kindness (חֶסֶד) is 72, which can also be expressed as $2 \cdot 6^2$, a number-form which is known in Kabbalah as a double-square. Double square numbers are most often found in relation to various (inherent) quantitative features of nature.[27] As such, the number 72 represents the perfected state of the 6 emotive attributes of the heart that correspond to the 6 days of creation. The factor of two multiplying 6^2 represents the perfect love and harmony within creation, "as one's face is reflected in water [the basic physical symbol of loving-kindness] so is the heart of man to man."[28] Similarly, the *Zohar*[29] speaks of 72 Bridges of Loving-kindness that connect together, in perfect harmony, all of created reality.

Gevurah: Might

Might is the fifth of the ten *sefirot*, and second of the emotive attributes in creation.

Might is associated with the power to restrain one's innate urge to bestow goodness upon others, when the recipient of that good is judged to be unworthy and liable to misuse it. As the force which measures, assesses the worthiness of creation, *gevurah* is also referred to in Kabbalah as the attribute of judgment (*midat hadin*).

It is the restraining quality of might that allows one to overcome one's enemies, be they from without or from within (i.e., one's evil inclination).

Loving-kindness and might act together to create an inner balance in one's attitude to one's environment. While loving-kindness seeks to draw others near, might reserves the option of repelling those deemed undeserving. As such, loving-kindness and might are the forces at work behind the sages saying: "The left-arm repels, while the right-arm draws near,"[30] and are thus seen to correspond to the right and left arms, respectively.

Though seemingly opposites, ultimately, it is the *sefirah* of might that manifests the power and forcefulness to implement one's innate desire for loving-kindness. Only by the power of the *sefirah* of might can loving-kindness penetrate the coarse, opposing surface of reality. The numerical value of the Hebrew name of might (גְּבוּרָה) is 216, which is three times the numerical value of loving-kindness (חֶסֶד), 72. In the Torah, the concept of anything occurring three times represents strength, or permanence.[31] Thus, a phenomenon that manifests or repeats itself three times becomes a firm and well-established reality. As such, might is indeed the affirmation of the reality of loving-kindness.

The numerical value of might, 216, is also a cube number: 6 · 6 · 6. In the Torah, the physical manifestations of this cube were the tablets of the covenant on which the Ten Commandments were carved that Moses received at Sinai, which were 6 by 6 by 6 handbreadths. Indeed, the sages describe that the Torah was given to Moses and Israel "from the Mouth of the Might [i.e., of God]."[32] It is most significant that the name of no other *sefirah* is used by the sages as a connotation for God Himself. In relation to the giving of the Torah, might implies God's essential ability to contract and concentrate His Infinite Light and strength into the finite letters of the Torah, especially those letters engraved on the tablets of the Ten Commandments.[33]

Figuratively, it is the two arms of loving-kindness and might together that serve God in creating all of reality. The numerical sum of the Hebrew names of loving-kindness (72) and might (216) is 288, which is also the number of the fallen sparks of holiness (from the primordial cataclysm of the breaking of the vessels) which permeate all of created reality, implying that our ability to perform the basic task of sifting through creation to redeem these sparks is undertaken with these two basic faculties of our soul. Through the dual effort of loving-kindness and might, these fallen sparks are redeemed and elevated to return and unite with their ultimate source. In a universal sense, this is the secret of the coming of the Messiah at the End of Days (primarily a manifestation of God's infinite loving-kindness) and the

Resurrection of the Dead (primarily a manifestation of God's infinite might).

Tiferet: Beauty

Beauty is the sixth of the ten *sefirot,* and the third of the emotive attributes within creation.

Beauty appears in the configuration of the *sefirot* along the middle axis, directly beneath knowledge (or beneath crown, when knowledge is excluded). It is associated with the power to reconcile conflicting inclinations, namely those of loving-kindness and might by finding their shared harmony, so as to allow for focused compassion. The compassionate nature that results out of the harmonious blend of loving-kindness with might accounts for beauty's designation in Kabbalah as the attribute of mercy (*midat harachamim*).

The Hebrew name of this *sefirah, tiferet,* is indeed a type of beauty. In Hebrew there are 8 different synonyms for beauty. More precisely, *tiferet* connotes the type of beauty that manifests itself through an elegant blend of emotive gestures implicit within its expression.

Together with loving-kindness and might (which it harmonizes) beauty forms the crux of the emotional realm. The numerical value of the Hebrew word *tiferet* is 1081 (the triangle of 46). With the other two primary emotional *sefirot,* the numerical value of these three *sefirot* is 72 + 216 + 1081 = 1369. 1369 is a perfect square (37^2), signifying that these three *sefirot* together exist in perfect inter-inclusion. Inter-inclusion, one of the most central concepts in Kabbalah and Chassdut, means that every part of a whole reflects all of its parts, a quality that is physically exhibited in a hologram. Thus, when in a harmonious state, the emotive realm exhibits a unity of purpose and calmness.

1369 is also the number of letters in the chapter of the Torah that precedes the Ten Commandments.[34] This chapter describes the preparation of Israel to receive the Torah at Sinai. Indeed, the

Torah itself corresponds to the *sefirah* of beauty and the Ten Commandments were given to Moses on two tablets with five commandments engraved upon each, corresponding to the five fingers of each of the Divine hands, the two *sefirot* of loving-kindness and might.

1369 is also the numerical value of the conclusion of the second verse of the Torah: "and the spirit of God hovered upon the face of the waters."[35] The Torah is usually likened to water as it travels downhill, from a high place (its seat with the Almighty) to a low place (our mundane reality). Thus, "the waters" in this phrase symbolize the Torah, while "God's spirit hovering upon the face of the waters" alludes to the Torah chapter that precedes the giving of the Torah and as noted, comprises 1369 letters.

Netzach: Victory

Victory is the seventh of the ten *sefirot,* and the first of the pragmatic or behavioral attributes within creation.

Victory is associated with the power to overcome those obstacles that stand in the way of realizing one's aspiration to bestow goodness upon creation. Insofar as the Hebrew name of this *sefirah* denotes both victory and eternity, it can be said that the ultimate victory enjoyed by a person is that over death itself, the final impediment to the pursuit of loving-kindness, the *sefirah* directly above victory, considered its source.

Before killing *Agag* the King of *Amalek*, the prophet Samuel said: "the Eternity of Israel [i.e., God] shall neither deceive nor regret, for He is not human that He may regret."[36] God here is called "the Eternity of Israel," *Netzach Yisrael.*[37] Unlike a human being who regrets, thereby changing his mind, the Almighty is eternal in the sense that His will and thought are eternal and never changing. From this verse and its description of the eternal, we learn that the *sefirah* of victory/eternity connotes standing firm and never regretting. As such, the power of the *sefirah* of victory/eternity is overcoming our mortal fear of death and thereby not entertaining regrets or doubts when faced with death.

As explained in Chassidut, moral and emotional clarity are specifically attainable at moments of *mesirut nefesh*, literally, a willingness to sacrifice one's own being for God. This epitome of Jewish will-power lies latent, as explained in the Tanya, in every Jewish soul and is associated with the *sefirah* of victory/eternity. The willingness to sacrifice one's own being stems out of the understanding that God's being is eternal ("the Eternity of Israel") and that by clinging to Him one is in touch with eternity.

Hod: Acknowledgment

Acknowledgment is the eighth of the ten *sefirot*, and the second pragmatic or behavioral attribute within creation. It is also closely linked with the *sefirah* of victory and in many ways they are considered a couple.

Acknowledgment is associated with the power to continually seek the realization of one's life goals with a determination and perseverance born out of a deep inner commitment.

The Hebrew word *hod* denotes acknowledgment, or splendor, or majesty. The acknowledgment of a supreme purpose in life inspires the total submission of self to that purpose. These are the two characteristics of a true leader or king and serve to endow one with an aura of splendor and majesty.[38] The sages relate that for the kings of the House of David, the ability to acknowledge a higher purpose translates into an actual physical trait. The truly suitable king was able to physically wear the special crown used by David, the crown fit him perfectly.[39] The notion of acknowledging a higher purpose, ties acknowledgment directly with the *sefirah* of crown, the source of higher, super-rational beliefs and ideals.

Acknowledgment also manifests as the power to express thanksgiving, or gratitude; in this capacity acknowledgment complements the giving attribute of the *sefirah* of loving-kindness.

As a pair, victory and acknowledgment are referred to in the *Zohar* as "two halves of a single body."[40] Often in Kabbalah they are considered as one *sefirah*. Indeed, in the human form they are seen to correspond to the right and left legs, which too can only perform their function of walking in unison.

Another symbol used for victory and acknowledgment together is that of scales of justice.[41] Whereas victory corresponds to the right scale, which accrues merits, acknowledgment is symbolized by the left scale, which symbolically concedes/acknowledges that everything we receive in life is not due to merit, but rather a gratis gift from God.

Yesod: Foundation

Foundation is the ninth of the ten *sefirot*, and the third of the behavioral or habitual attributes. Foundation is associated with the power to contact, connect, and communicate with external reality, which in Kabbalah is represented by the *sefirah* of kingdom. To use a physical analogy, the foundation of a building grounds, or connects it with its environs, making sure that it does not move.

In the body, foundation is identified with the procreative organs and serves to ground the individual to the world by ensuring his or her continuation in the generations to come. Chassidic teachings explain that the ability to procreate manifests an infinite power within the finite context of the created human being. As such, foundation is referred to as the small limb of man, the "minute [in quantity] that holds the large [the infinite, in quality]."[42]

Indeed, each individual person is minute relative to all the generations that will be born from him. Foundation is also the small and narrow bridge between the infinite potential of procreation that flows into it and its actual manifestation in the progeny of man. For this reason, the *sefirah* of foundation is identified in the Torah with the *tzadik*, the holy, righteous individual, as the Proverbs teach: "the *tzadik* is the foundation of the world."[43] In particular, this refers to the one, consummate *tzadik* of the generation. In the very body of the *tzadik*, which is finite and limited in time and space, God's Infinite Light and creative life-force become manifest. The *tzadik* procreates on the spiritual plane as well as on the physical plane. He experiences procreation in the inner eye of his consciousness, in the continual flow of new insights and true innovations in the study and understanding of the Torah. His procreative power also arouses and inspires the souls of his generation to return to God and the Torah.

Foundation is also referred to as the covenant (*brit*), referring, in particular, to the covenant of circumcision that God made with Abraham. In Kabbalah, it refers to the covenant enjoining the two Divine attributes of truth (*emet*) and peace (*shalom*), of which the prophet says, "Truth and peace shall you love."[44] Truth is the inner experiential quality of the *sefirah* of foundation, while peace is the gift that God gives to the *sefirah* of foundation (i.e., to one who has rectified his power of foundation).[45]

In particular, Abraham represents the origin of love in the soul. God described Abraham as "the one who loves Me."[46] Energetically, all of Abraham's loving-kindness flows down (as water) to become concentrated in foundation. There it creates the covenant between the absolute truth of the Torah and the peace that results from good deeds of the *tzadik*, performed with love for Israel.

Malchut: Kingdom

Kingdom is the last of the ten *sefirot*, and appears in the configuration of the *sefirot* at the bottom of the middle axis, directly beneath foundation.

Kingdom is associated with the power of expression, therefore it is often referred to as the world of speech insofar as the spoken word represents the essential medium of self-expression, allowing one not only to reveal himself to others but to guide and influence them as well. Hence, speech allows one to exercise authority and kingship, the literal meaning of the Hebrew word *malchut*.

Kingdom also serves as the means for establishing identification with outer reality. Exercising kingship requires utmost sensitivity to the needs of the realm that one seeks to rule.

Hence, kingdom demands that every agent of influence within creation also consider itself to be a recipient *vis a vis* the Divine source of all authority, for only then can the ultimate good of the physical realm be assured. One can only ascend to the higher *sefirot* through the portal of kingdom. "This is the gate that leads to God, the righteous shall pass through it."[47] In one's devoted service to God, this means receiving upon oneself, in total commitment, "the yoke of the kingdom of heaven."

The numerical value of the Hebrew word *malchut* (מַלְכוּת) is 496, which is the triangle of 31, i.e., the sum of all numbers from 1 to 31. In addition to being a triangular number, 496 is a "perfect number," that is, a number which equals the sum of all of its divisors. (The first four "perfect numbers" are 1, 6, 28, 496.) Thus, the ten *sefirot* reach their consummate end with a perfect number.

In summary, these are the *sefirot* and their powers:

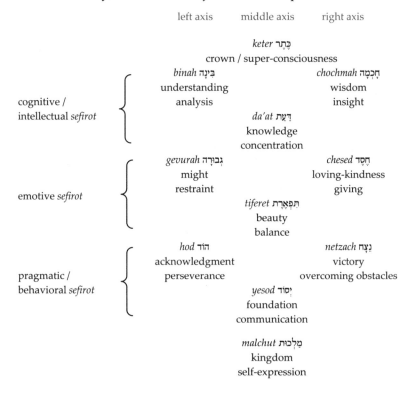

	left axis	middle axis	right axis
		keter כֶּתֶר	
		crown / super-consciousness	
	binah בִּינָה		*chochmah* חָכְמָה
	understanding		wisdom
cognitive /	analysis		insight
intellectual *sefirot*		*da'at* דַּעַת	
		knowledge	
		concentration	
	gevurah גְּבוּרָה		*chesed* חֶסֶד
	might		loving-kindness
emotive *sefirot*	restraint		giving
		tiferet תִּפְאֶרֶת	
		beauty	
		balance	
	hod הוֹד		*netzach* נֶצַח
	acknowledgment		victory
pragmatic /	perseverance		overcoming obstacles
behavioral *sefirot*		*yesod* יְסוֹד	
		foundation	
		communication	
		malchut מַלְכוּת	
		kingdom	
		self-expression	

Notes:

1. Exodus 24:10 and Ezekiel 1:26, 10:1.

2. Based on a letter written by the Ba'al Shem Tov, the founder of Chassidut. See in length in the introduction to *The Hebrew Letters*.

3. The image of the ladder is based on Jacob's ladder described in Genesis 28:12. Usually, the four-runged latter that Jacob saw symbolizes the Four Worlds we will discuss later. Thus, the ladder serves as a link between the model of the *sefirot* and the model of the Worlds illustrated in the chart on p. 135.

4. Based on the major collection of the Arizal's teachings, titled *Eitz Chaim, The Tree of Life*.

5. Genesis 1:26.

6. See *Body, Mind, and Soul*, pp. 24 and 74 for the charts of the *sefirot* and their corresponding organs and physiological systems.

7. The question arises whether God's choice of how to reveal Himself reflects His true essence, in which case, though we cannot fathom His essence, we can gather something about it from the Torah, the blueprint of all that is, or, whether the prism that God choses does not reflect His essence. In Kabbalah, this question remains open. In Chassidut, the former view is openly condoned, making in the end for a stronger feeling of the imminence rather than the absolute transcendence of the Almighty. This topic is covered in length in the article *"Shlosha Chushim"* (Three Intuitions) in the Hebrew volume, *Esa Einai*.

8. Exodus 34:6-7. Later, the Almighty revealed Himself again to Moses through a similar set of 9 Divine attributes (Numbers 14:18). On the relationship between the 13 Divine attributes and the 9 Divine attributes, see in depth in the Hebrew volume *Emunah Umuda'oot (Faith and Consciousness)*. Let it suffice here to say that together the 13 and the 9 correspond to the 22 letters of the Hebrew alphabet.

9. One of the first times that the relation of the ten *sefirot* to the thirteen attributes of Divine mercy is mentioned in a well-documented source, is the enigmatic query addressed to Rav Hai Gaon, one of the sages of the Gaonite period (9th century CE), by

his disciples: "We know 10 [sefirot], but we do not know 13" (see Rabbi Moses Cordovero, *Pardes Rimonim* 1:7).

10. *Mishnah Avot* 5:1. *Rosh Hashanah* 32a. The Magid of Mezritch states that the Ten Utterances with which God created the world correspond to the Ten Commandments, with which He gave the Torah that rectifies the world. For more on this correspondence see *The Art of Education*, pp. 237ff.

11. *Tanya, Sha'ar Hayichud Veha'emunah*, chs. 11-12. For an explanation of these three concepts—light, life-force, and energy—see the introduction to *The Hebrew Letters*, pp. 2ff.

12. These seven commandments are: washing hands before meals (נְטִילַת יָדַיִם), enclosing communities for Shabbat (עֵירוּבִין), blessings before food, commandments, and special occasions (בְּרָכוֹת), lighting Shabbat candles (שַׁבָּת), reading the Book of Esther on Purim (מְגִלָּה), lighting Chanukah candles (חֲנֻכָּה), and praising God by reciting chapters 113-118 of Psalms on special occasions (הַלֵּל). All seven can be easily remembered with the mnemonic acronym: נָע בְּשִׂמְחָה, pronounced *na besimchah*, and which means "moves joyfully."

13. Exodus 20:2-14.

14. In fact, there is a Chassidic commentary on the Five Books of Moses—*Heichal Habrachah*, by the Komarna Rebbe—that explains the correspondence of each particular letter to the Torah's commandments, as they appear.

15. Psalms 104:24.

16. Genesis 1:1.

17. Job 12:11, 34:3. In a beautiful example of self-reference, the initials of the words: "The ear examines words," in Hebrew (אֹזֶן מִלִּין תִּבְחָן) form the word אמת—truth!

18. Deuteronomy 6:4.

19. Genesis 37:37. I Chronicles 1:48.

20. See *Zohar* III, 4a.

21. The Hebrew word *da'at* can be translated into English as "knowledge," "consciousness," or "perspective." See p. 67, note 4.

22. *Zohar (Sifra Detzni'uta)* II, 177a.

23. The numerical values of the Hebrew words for "one" and "love" are both 13.

24. Psalms 42:9.

25. *Zohar* III, 191b.

26. *Ibid.* I, 46a.

27. The most striking example being that they are the fundamental numbers underlying the periodicity of the Periodic Table of the elements. This topic will be covered in depth in a forthcoming volume on Kabbalah and Science.

28. Proverbs 27:19.

29. *Zohar* III, 227a.

30. *Sotah* 47a.

31. *Bava Metzi'a* 106b. The numerical value of this word in Hebrew, חֶזְקָה, is 120, the number of years in a consummate lifetime. 120 divides into 3 itself, 120 = 3 · 40, thus, the consummate life comprises three 40 years phases; each period of 40 years represents another stage of the "pleasure of being alive."

    Moses passed away on his 120th birthday. His life consisted of three distinct "phases," or "lifetimes," each lasting 40 years; therefore he is considered to have a "permanence" of life. That is one reason for why the *Zohar* says that Moses did not pass away, he is merely hidden from our sight, just as the moon does not cease to exist but is only hidden from our sight once a month (*Zohar* I, 37b-38a, and elsewhere).

32. *Makot* 24a. In Hebrew, the numerical value of the phrase "from the Mouth of the Might" (מִפִּי הַגְּבוּרָה) is 351, the triangle of 26, the value of God's essential Name, *Havayah*. In Chassidut it is explained that "Might" connotes God's unique ability to carry opposites, which in the Giving of the Torah manifests as His ability to permeate the finite letters and words of the Torah with His infinite light and essence.

33. As noted by various commentaries, that the Ten Commandments allude to all 613 commandments of the Torah. See *Rashi* to Exodus 25:12. See also footnote 14, above.

34. Exodus chapter 19 and the first verse of chapter 20.

35. Genesis 1:2.

36. 1 Samuel 15:29.

37. God here is not referred to by the word "eternity" alone, but by the composite idiom "the Eternity of Israel." As noted above, only the name of the *sefirah* of might is used as a direct connotation for God. Nonetheless, eternity, which also means "victory," and might are connected, as they are the two *sefirot* that relate to the supernatural power to overcome war or conflict, i.e., to the Divine power to overcome the trials and tribulations of this world.

38. See *The Art of Education*, pp. 249-50.

39. *Avodah Zarah* 44a-b. According to Rashi the royal crown had a bar spanning its diameter on the inside, and could only be worn by a person with a corresponding recess in his skullbone (*Rashi* to the words *shebikesh leholmo velo holamto* in *Sanhedrin* 21b).

40. *Zohar* III, 236a.

41. *Sha'arei Ahavah Veratzon* (Gates of Love and Will), p. 225.

42. See *Bereisheet Rabbah* 5:7

43. Proverbs 10:25.

44. Zachariah 8:19. The initials of "truth" (אֱמֶת) and "peace" (שָׁלוֹם) spell the Hebrew word for "fire" (אֵשׁ). Since foundation is the *sefirah* of covenants, these initials allude to the first word of the Bible, "In the beginning" (בְּרֵאשִׁית), whose letters are explained in the *Tikunei Zohar* to be a permutation of the two words "a covenant of fire" (בְּרִית אֵשׁ). Thus, the entire Torah begins with this idea.

    Even more amazingly, when the value of "truth" (אֱמֶת = 441) and "peace" (שָׁלוֹם = 376) is added to the word "fire" (אֵשׁ = 301) the sum is 1118, the numerical value of the *Shema*, the quintessential statement of Jewish faith in the Unity of the Almighty: שְׁמַע יִשְׂרָאֵל יהו־ה אֱ־לֹהֵינוּ יהו־ה אֶחָד = 1118, indicating the centrality of truth and peace in the covenant made between God and the Jewish people.

45. Indeed, *Sefer Yetzirah* (4:1) reveals that one who does not keep one's covenant transforms peace, the gift of foundation, into war.

46. Isaiah 41:8.

47. Psalms 118:20.

Sefirot and the Soul

7

EACH OF THE *SEFIROT* POSSESSES BOTH AN EXTERNAL AS WELL AS AN internal dimension. The external dimension and characteristics of each *sefirah*—as described above—is identified with the functional role that the *sefirah* plays in the process of creation. The *sefirah's* internal dimension is identified with the hidden motivational force that inspires its activity. This inner dimension can only be appreciated in context of how it manifests itself in the soul and thus gives us the context for looking at the *sefirot* in relation to the dimension of the soul. Given the soul's Divine origin, we can understand how an analysis of its essential characteristics can serve as the best vehicle for achieving insight into the meaning of the ten *sefirot*.

While the Kabbalistic names of the *sefirot* serve well to express the effect that each of these channels of Divine energy has upon creation, in order to properly describe the function of the *sefirot* in the context of the soul, a more experiential, or psychological terminology is employed. This terminology was first developed by Kabbalistic masters, but found its final form in the writings of the Chassidic masters. As we shall see, the terminology used to name each *sefirah* from the perspective of its inner experiential character perfectly parallels and reveals its essential nature.

Let us begin by presenting the full chart of the *sefirot* and their internal experiential manifestations.

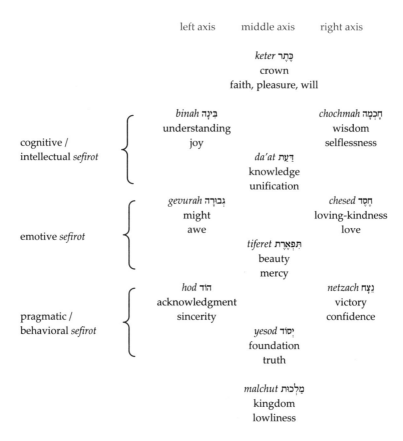

left axis   middle axis   right axis

keter כֶּתֶר
crown
faith, pleasure, will

cognitive /
intellectual *sefirot*

binah בִּינָה
understanding
joy

chochmah חׇכְמָה
wisdom
selflessness

da'at דַּעַת
knowledge
unification

emotive *sefirot*

gevurah גְּבוּרָה
might
awe

chesed חֶסֶד
loving-kindness
love

tiferet תִּפְאֶרֶת
beauty
mercy

pragmatic /
behavioral *sefirot*

hod הוֹד
acknowledgment
sincerity

netzach נֶצַח
victory
confidence

yesod יְסוֹד
foundation
truth

malchut מַלְכוּת
kingdom
lowliness

Crown: Faith, Pleasure, and Will

Much like the intricate design of the crown of a king, so is the *sefirah* of crown described in the *Zohar* as comprising three heads.[1] Each head symbolizes a different level of the super-conscious.

The highest of these is called the unknowable head (*radla*, in the Hebrew acronym), and it is expressed in the soul as the experience of faith. The second head of the crown is termed the head of nothingness (*reisha d'ayin*), and its inner experience in the soul is pleasure. The third head is called the long, extended head (*reisha d'arich*), and it manifests in the soul as the experience of will, or will-power.[2]

Let us take a moment to look at these three manifestations of the crown: faith, pleasure, and will.

Faith (*emunah*) is the essential connection, or covenant, between Israel and God.[3] Chassidut teaches that the simple faith of the simple Jew links him or her to the simple (absolute) unity of God's very essence. Every Jewish soul inherits its faith from the patriarchs and matriarchs of the Jewish people; in particular, from Abraham, the "first [monotheistic] believer."[4] As an inherited trait, faith is always present in every Jewish soul, though not necessarily conscious.[5]

While the source of Jewish faith comes from the patriarchs, it was the function of Moses to sustain and reinforce the consciousness of the faith of Israel, and hence Jewish identity. Just as a body needs physical sustenance to stay alive, so the faith inherent in every Jewish soul requires the figurative food of the Torah's wisdom in order to thrive.[6] Thus, in the *Zohar*, Moses is known as the faithful shepherd (*ra'aya mehemna*), which also means, the shepherd of faith. In the wanderings of the Jewish people in the desert the heavenly manna, which provided spiritual as well as physical sustenance, was given in the merit of Moses.[7]

Just as every Jewish soul is permeated with the faith of Abraham, each one is also permeated with the guiding wisdom of Moses. As explained in Chassidut, every Jew has a spark of the soul of Moses in him or her, which makes it possible for faith to be practically put to work in daily life.[8] In addition, in every generation there is a *tzadik* who in Kabbalah is referred to as "the extension of Moses,"[9] a particular leader who serves the same function as Moses, strengthening the true faith of monotheism.

Pleasure (*ta'anug*), as it is manifested in crown is not a reaction to stimulation from a source external to the soul. Instead it is an energetic source for the soul, namely it is the life force, the fluid or living waters, of all the soul's powers. The crown's pleasure particularly serves to motivate and direct super-conscious will.

Will power, completely super-rational in itself, serves to control and direct (from above and without) all of the conscious powers of the soul, starting with the intellect, the soul's base of rationality. Once the rational mind is active, a lower level of will power serves as the soul's source for the energy needed to willfully pursue those objectives rationally chosen by the mind.

God's higher will finds its essential expression in the commandments given to Israel in the Torah. When we devotedly fulfill God's commandments purely because they are the expression of His essential will, we connect ourselves to His higher will. Devotion and acting devotedly are thus human expressions of God's higher will. By performing God's commandments for rational reasons, for instance, basing one's practice upon the secrets revealed to us in Kabbalah with regard to the spiritual effects of each commandment in particular, we connect ourselves to the lower level of God's will.

Wisdom: Selflessness, or Self-Nullification

Selflessness (bitul) is the experiential state associated with wisdom. Selflessness does not just govern our interactions with other people, but first and foremost our relationship with God. With respect to God, selflessness does not mean doing something for Him, but rather maintaining a state of rectified being. Normally our state of mind is such that we seem to be autonomous beings, separate and independent from everything around us, including God. Selflessness in respect to God means nullifying our sense of being a separate entity—reducing our consciousness of self to naught—and feeling how we are actually one with the Almighty. Through selflessness we open our consciousness to a continuous flow of Divine wisdom and insight, and thereby become aware of our true potential as part of the Divine plan.[10]

Chassidut identifies two levels of selflessness, or nullification of the self. The first, considered the absolute form of self-nullification, is called nullification of reality, whereby one loses all sense of his or her independent existence. The second is called nullification of ego, whereby while still feeling oneself separate from God, one is actively engaged in the process of consciously nullifying his or her external layer of self/ego. This is accomplished by meditation on the continual recreation of all reality, including oneself, and the concentrated effort to experience one's own ego, which itself is continually being recreated "something from nothing," as totally dependent on the Divine "nothing," the cause of its existence. The result of this spiritual effort is the realization that there is no independent reality other than God, a realization that serves to diminish the domain of the ego in one's psyche.

Understanding: Joy

Joy (*simchah*) is the spiritual state associated with the *sefirah* of understanding. Joy comes from the spiritual satisfaction of having succeeded in comprehending an idea and relating it to one's emotions (eliciting emotional response). In Kabbalah, understanding is associated with motherhood,[11] of which the Bible says, "The mother of the children is joyful."[12]

The joy of motherhood develops in progressive stages. First there is the joy of betrothal and marriage, which extends into the joy of anticipating pregnancy (a state of mind which actually facilitates conception). Then follows the joy of conceiving, which extends throughout the pregnancy into the joy of expecting birth. Finally, "The mother of the children is joyful" because of the children she has borne, a joy that extends into her looking forward to raising them.

Thus, though each joyous moment is the result of a particular stage of accomplishment, it also includes an anticipation for something more, a looking forward to the next stage.[13] This future anticipation associated with the experiential joy of the *sefirah* of understanding helps to define the nature of understanding in Kabbalah. *Sefer Yetzirah* describes the *sefirot* as metaphysical depths of reality. There, the *sefirah* of understanding is known as the depth of the future, an identification that is followed in the *Zohar*, which describes the inner experience of understanding as the joyous experience of the World to Come.

The three festivals of the Jewish year—Passover, Shavu'ot, and Sukot—are the source of our experience of joy throughout the year. In Kabbalah, each of these festivals is likened to a different stage of feminine development, which itself corresponds to one of the three different stages of joy described above. The joy of Passover is likened to a daughter, which corresponds to the joy of betrothal and marriage and the consequent anticipation of conception. The joy of Shavu'ot, the celebration of the giving of the Torah at Mt. Sinai, is likened to the experience of being a sister (a feeling of partnership with one's husband, as sister to brother), which reveals the joy of conception entailing the expectation of birth. Finally, the joy of Sukot is described as the experience of being a mother, and hence corresponds to the joy of birth and the dedication to raising one's family. The joy of Sukot concludes with the celebration of Simchat Torah, "the joy of the Torah," implying that the consummate joy of motherhood involves building a home that celebrates God's greatest gift to us: His Torah.

Knowledge: Unification

Unification (yichud) is the experiential state of the soul associated with the sefirah of knowledge. As explained in Chassidut, knowledge means unification, particularly that of two bodies or souls. Of the union of man and wife, the Torah says: "He [the male] shall cling to his wife and they shall become one flesh."[14] This verse follows God's creating Adam and Eve (from Adam's own body). Subsequently, the Torah describes the physical union of Adam and Eve as an act of knowledge: "And Adam knew his wife Eve."[15]

The power of unification is rooted in the soul's experience of the sefirah of knowledge. On this experience hinges one's ability to recognize his or her soul mate and establish with that person an authentic rapport. Unification is thus the process of bringing back together the two lost halves of what was initially a single entity.[16]

Unification occurs at all levels of reality. The source of the experience of unification between two people is in the corresponding spiritual unification that occurs in the spiritual realm. Kabbalah, especially as taught by the Arizal, interprets the content of the traditional Jewish prayers in terms of unifications (that prayer facilitates) between spiritual entities that affect the physical realm. These unifications are known as *kavanot* or mystical intentions.[17,18]

Loving-kindness: Love

Love (*ahavah*) is the experiential state associated with the *sefirah* of loving-kindness. God created the world with love and sustains the world with love, and, therefore, love is the essential power of growth[19] inherent throughout reality. The experience of love begins with a sense of attraction and being drawn to another, a sense that continues to grow and expand until it virtually encompasses one and one's beloved. Love can be pictured as an attractive vector force, flowing from one entity to another.[20]

The numerical value of the word "love" in Hebrew (אַהֲבָה) is 13. Chassidic teachings note that there are 13 different types of love, which we will present here in chart form as they align and correspond with the *sefirot* (note also how, as mentioned above, the ten *sefirot* expand into 13), as follows:

עַתִּיק – פְּנִימִיּוּת הַכֶּתֶר
Atik – internal facet of crown
the love of God for Israel

אֲרִיךְ – חִיצוֹנִיּוּת הַכֶּתֶר
Arich – external facet of crown
the love of Israel for God

בִּינָה   חָכְמָה
understanding   wisdom
the love of a student for his teacher   *the love of a teacher for his student*

דַּעַת
knowledge
the love between students

גְּבוּרָה   חֶסֶד
might   loving-kindness
the love of a woman for her husband   *the love of a man for his wife*

תִּפְאֶרֶת
beauty
the love between friends

הוֹד   נֶצַח
acknowledgment   victory
the love of a child for his/her parent   *the love of a parent for his/her child*

יְסוֹד
foundation
the love between siblings

פְּנִימִיּוּת הַמַּלְכוּת
internal facet of kingdom
the love of a king for his subjects

חִיצוֹנִיּוּת הַמַּלְכוּת
external facet of kingdom
the love of subjects for their king

Of all these 13 types of love, the love between God and Israel is the most essential. The Torah teaches that love for God passes through three incremental stages, which are described in the verse: "And you shall love *God* your God with all of your heart, and with all of your soul, and with all of your might."[21] Because love for God is the most essential of all the types of love, it defines the nature of all the others. Thus, just as love for God develops in three stages, so do each of the other types of love. The discussion of how each develops is of course beyond our scope here.[22]

Might: Awe

Fear, or awe (*yirah*), is the inner dimension of the *sefirah* of might, as it is experienced in the soul. In contrast to the heart's innate desire to give, which derives from love, fear expresses one's deeply felt apprehension that one's gift may fall into the hands of an unworthy recipient who may actually misuse it destructively. Fear evokes the might necessary to reject and even fight against negative and destructive forces.

In a more general sense, fear is understood to represent one's sensitivity to the presence of another. Sensitivity gives rise to consideration of the other's feelings and respect for him or her. With respect comes a sense of distance, not to interfere with the other. So, while love motivates attraction and closeness, fear stands in awe from afar.

In relation to God, there are many levels of fear, which in general are categorized under two separate headings: awe and fear. Awe is usually the result of intellectual understanding, such as when one realizes that one is standing in the presence of God's infinite Being. Fear usually results from an emotional realization, such as the experience that one may have of the fear of punishment that follows God's justice. Fear of punishment is not completely pure in its motivation. It does not relate to God directly as the object of one's perception or comprehension, but rather derives from an indirect experience of the Divine. Therefore, it involves a mixture of good and evil: good, by deterring the person from performing negative acts, and evil, because it shadows one's consciousness with thoughts of bad consequences.

The two powers of love and fear complement one another and act as a pair, as the two hands of the body in their common effort to construct. In the *Zohar*, love and awe are likened to the two wings of a bird in its flight upward. This metaphor is meant to stress that without love and awe, the two archetypal emotional experiences, the worship of God, and specifically the performance of His commandments, remains grounded, unable to lift-up spiritually.

Beauty: Mercy

Mercy (*rachamim*) is the experiential state associated with the *sefirah* of beauty. Compassion synthesizes the apparently opposite forces of love and fear—the desire to give and the demand to withhold.

Love considers everything and everyone as a potential recipient of its benevolence. Fear first judges each potential recipient, determining whether he or she or it is worthy of receiving the benevolence. Mercy allows true empathy for others, by considering them in the context of their present life situations; it penetrates beneath and beyond superficial objectivity. In this vein, the sages describe God judging creation on *Rosh Hashanah* (the New Year) as seemingly standing up from the throne of severe judgment and sitting down, as it were, on the throne of mercy.[23]

Although the gifts of pure love and loving-kindness may be quantitatively greater than those of mercy, giving out of an experience of mercy is qualitatively richer. By mercy, we give our very selves to others for our empathy with them is so great that we feel that they are an actual extension of ourselves.

Victory: Confidence

Confidence (*bitachon*) is the experiential state associated with the *sefirah* of victory.

Chassidic teachings identify two types of confidence: active and passive. Active confidence is the confidence we possess in our own ability to succeed in life. Passive confidence is the trust that we have in Divine Providence that things will turn out well.

The active confidence of victory represents the power of the soul to take initiative. God desires of us independent initiative—

the initiative to rectify all that lies within our sphere of influence. But, in taking initiative, we must continually recognize that it is God who desires and inspires our taking initiative and that it is He who gives us the power to succeed and acheive.[24] Without the continual influx of His life force and energy we would remain powerless.

As a Jew, one's confidence to take initiative is accompanied with the sense of one's being a part of the eternal people, the people of God, "the Eternity of Israel,"[25] the people who in the end will be victorious over all those that oppose them and all obstacles that stand in their way, even over the angel of death. Confidence entails the ability to envision how our dreams will come true—in its essence, a minor form of prophecy. As explained in Kabbalah, the source of prophecy is in the *sefirot* of victory/eternity and acknowledgment.[26] Eternity manifests the soul's power to endow our children with a holy feeling of self-confidence, as "the son is his father's thigh,"[27] the thigh being part of the bodily manifestation of eternity, or victory, as will be explained.

Acknowledgment: Sincerity

Sincerity (*temimut*) is the experiential state associated with the *sefirah* of acknowledgment. The Hebrew word *temimut* is often translated as naiveté, just as a child is naturally naive. It is the ability to retain a child's seemingly naive and direct outlook on life that allows a person to live his life in a state of sincerity. Without sincerity, doubt and cynicism dampen and ridicule one's trust and confidence in the Almighty and in one's ability to truly be successful in growing closer to Him. So, just as acknowledgment complements victory and together they are considered two sides of the same coin, so the experiential state of sincerity complements that of confidence.

There are three general levels of sincerity: sincerity of will; sincerity of heart; and sincerity of action. In Hebrew, sincerity (*temimut*) implies completeness. Thus, sincerity of will means that one is fully committed to fulfill God's will. This type of sincere commitment does not necessarily penetrate the soul's emotional realm or make its mark on all of one's actions.

Sincerity of heart is the complete devotion of all one's experience to serving God. What this means is that regardless of the situation that one finds oneself in and the emotional experience that the situation evokes, one's heart is singularly directed and devoted to serving the Almighty.

At the level of action, sincerity represents our sense of down to earth commitment and dedication to meticulously fulfill each and every detail of God's commandments.

Chassidut teaches that of all the emotions of the heart, sincerity, in all its aspects, is an innate gift of God, the hardest attribute to be acquired through conscious effort. It is indeed the most essential attribute of the Jewish people.[28] Throughout the Bible, sincerity appears as an idiom together with the verb "to walk."[29] With sincerity, God's chosen people can walk in His ways and, in essence, walk with Him.

Foundation: Truth

Truth (*emet*) is the experiential state of the soul manifested by the *sefirah* of foundation.

According to the sages, "the seal of the Almighty is truth."[30] Thus, truth refers to a "concluding, sealing principle," as we will explain. It is as if truth acts as a sealant. The final Hebrew letters of the three words that conclude the account of creation— בָּרָא אֱלֹהִים לַעֲשׂוֹת, "God created to do"[31]—spell אֱמֶת, truth. God created reality "to do," which means that it is incumbent upon us, God's intelligent creatures, to complete the "doing," that is, seek the fulfillment of creation by rectifying it. And, the seal of creation, the instrument of fulfillment, is truth.

Additionally, the Hebrew word for truth, אֱמֶת, is described by the sages as comprising the first, middle, and last letters of the Hebrew alphabet, thus linking it with God's plan for creation, beginning with His will (symbolized by the first letter, א, *alef*), followed by the ongoing act of creation (symbolized by the letter מ, *mem*), and culminating with His seal (or Divine signature) being reflected and recognized in everything (symbolized by the letter ת, *tav*, whose name literally means a stamp or a seal).

As an emotional state of the soul, truth is understood to be the experience of the soul's impulsive drive that comes at the climax of a creative pursuit. This drive seeks to make the purpose of the pursuit come true; where victory was the ability to stand up and take initiative, envisioning one's future success, truth provides the power and drive to make one's efforts succeed in the here and now. Truth thus entails the experience of self-fulfillment in all of life's endeavors. Indeed, truth is the power to realize our deepest potential, which is in fact the power of the soul to bring about the ultimate realization of God's infinite potential.

Kingdom: Lowliness

Lowliness (*shiflut*) is the experiential state associated with the *sefirah* of kingdom.

In contrast to selflessness (the experiential state of wisdom), lowliness does not imply the negation of self, but rather the experience of oneself as existentially distant from God. It is said that, "From afar, God appears to me."[32] God's very essence is revealed to the person who feels distant from Him, more so than to the person who feels close to Him. Close and far here are not meant objectively, for just as every positive number (no matter how large) is equally smaller than infinity, so every individual, regardless of how pious and righteous, is infinitely far from the Almighty's infinite Being. Lowliness also serves as the ultimate motivation to return to God, for when God appears from afar one is aroused to approach and embrace Him. And indeed, God reveals His essence to the one who is ever returning to Him.

The Ba'al Shem Tov teaches that the beginning of all Divine service (the gateway of the *sefirah* of kingdom, as explained above) is to experience an existential sense of identification with even the most lowly of creatures on earth, as though saying, "they all fulfill

God's purpose and design faithfully; were only I able to do the same."

Being that lowliness is the experience of kingdom, it also serves as the defining characteristic of every true leader, regardless of the size of the group being lead. As related regarding King David, the true king is able to realize his sovereignty constructively in direct proportion to the depth of his existential state of lowliness. Indeed, as we saw earlier,[33] the Hebrew words for low tide (*shefel*) and high tide (*geut*), symbolic of a leader's lowliness and sovereignty, are numerically equal.

The *Sefirot* and the Human Body

Just as the ten *sefirot* can be seen manifest in the soul, so can they be seen manifest in the human body. Elsewhere we have explored models revealing the manifestation of the *sefirot* in the human body, including some models dealing with particular organs.[34] Here we will present the most straightforward model, which has been the staple of the study of Kabbalah for generations.

Crown is manifest in the body as the skull. Just as a crown encircles the head, so the skull encircles the brain. The skull further suggests the idea of placing a physical border on our field of conscious experience. Like consciousness, which is always surrounded by a border of unconscious experience that bounds it, the brain is surrounded by a physical barrier limiting its ability to expand.

In Kabbalah, wisdom, the father principle, is considered to be the essential power of the mind, or the mind within the mind, while understanding, the mother principle, is regarded as the heart within the mind. Mind is identified with water, while heart is identified with fire. Mind is cool, calm, and collected, while heart is hot, enamored, and passionate. Wisdom, the mind within the mind, is the intellect's cooler side, while understanding, the heart within the mind, is the intellect's warmer side. This distinction also plays itself out in the body, where wisdom is identified with the right lobe of the brain and understanding with the left lobe. The right lobe is more intuitive and insightful (water), while the left lobe is more analytic and critical (fire). The right lobe of the brain oversees the lungs, the water cooler of the body, while the left lobe of the brain oversees the heart, the fiery blood pump of the body. In the *Zohar* we find that without the cooling effect of the lungs on the heart, the heart would burn itself up.[35]

Knowledge, which also translates as "consciousness" and acts as a bridge between the mind and the heart, is identified with the rear lobe of the brain at the point where the brain meets the spine—the position of the occipital lobe.

With regard to the three emotional properties of the soul, we find that the right arm embodies loving-kindness and the left arm embodies might. This is alluded to in the verse from The Song of Songs,[36] "His left arm is under my head, and his right arm embraces me." As related above regarding these two *sefirot*, in certain contexts the sages prescribe that the left arm should repel, while the right arm should draw near. In this context the left arm grants others a sense of independence, the metaphorical meaning of "under my head," before the right arm seeks to draw them near, "embraces me."

The balancing power in the *sefirah* of beauty—identified with the torso—holds together all the parts of the body.

Victory and acknowledgment, the behavioral *sefirot*, correspond to the right and left legs, respectively. The legs represent the first and most continual contact with outer reality (the earth). Moreover, the legs facilitate the movement of the body as a whole, bringing a person where he or she wants to go. Victory portrays the quality of putting one's best foot forward in an assertive posture, and thus corresponds to the right leg, which is the more dominant of the legs. Acknowledgment, which corresponds to the left leg, keeps a person's movement on course by monitoring and validating his or her assertive thrust.

Foundation corresponds to the male and female reproductive organs, which lie between the two legs. Referred to as the "conclusion of the body,"[37] foundation is the body's *hidden* source and undercurrent of all physical manifestation (similar to the underground foundation of a building) and its ability to actualize and fulfill itself through procreation. Just as the crown is described as the unmovable mover, the unchanging Divine source of all change, so foundation is the unrevealed revealer—the source of the soul's ability to express itself, which itself is never openly expressed.

The last *sefirah*, kingdom manifests in the mouth. With speech we create our domain of influence. "The word of the king is his authority,"[38] meaning that the extent of any leader's rule is marked by how far his word travels.[39] The ability of the mouth to speak, to produce self-expression, is the power to affect one's environment, one's world. The ruling quality of speech is clearly illustrated by the fact that in order to create the world, the Almighty spoke, as described in the first chapter of Genesis.

Summarizing the correspondence between the *sefirot* and the human body, we have:

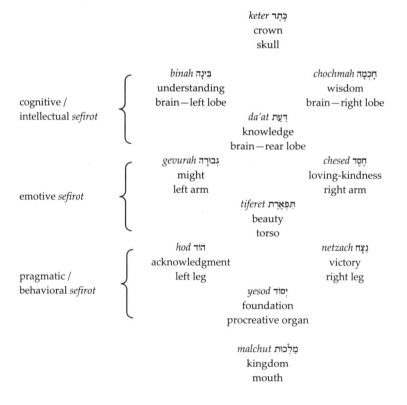

keter כֶּתֶר
crown
skull

cognitive /
intellectual *sefirot*

binah בִּינָה
understanding
brain—left lobe

chochmah חָכְמָה
wisdom
brain—right lobe

da'at דַּעַת
knowledge
brain—rear lobe

emotive *sefirot*

gevurah גְּבוּרָה
might
left arm

chesed חֶסֶד
loving-kindness
right arm

tiferet תִּפְאֶרֶת
beauty
torso

pragmatic /
behavioral *sefirot*

hod הוֹד
acknowledgment
left leg

netzach נֵצַח
victory
right leg

yesod יְסוֹד
foundation
procreative organ

malchut מַלְכוּת
kingdom
mouth

The *Sefirot* and the *Partzufim*

The *partzufim*, which literally mean personae (singular, *partzuf*), form a highly complex Kabbalistic model in which the *sefirot* metamorphose into human-like figures or personalities. Each *partzuf* possesses a full set of intellectual, emotive, and behavioral powers and is characterized by its ability to combine disparate elements into a unified whole, which is why each possesses a full set of ten *sefirot* of its own that continue to develop into 613 individual components, just as in the process of a seminal unit developing into a full human the human stature (containing 248 limbs and 365 sinews; $248 + 365 = 613$).

Unlike the *sefirot* whose interconnections and interactions are relatively easy to understand (lower levels evolving naturally from higher levels), higher level *partzufim* relate to lower level *partzufim* by a much more mysterious relationship called enclothement or incarnation, just as a soul enters a body.

The *partzufim* and their interactions are too complex to be treated with rigor in an introductory text on Kabbalah. It is only the most difficult and mysterious sections of the *Zohar* that contain an exposition on their nature. One might ask: if indeed the *partzufim* present such an elaborate model, how are they useful? The answer is that *partzufim* form part of a more advanced way of analyzing reality. Without them, most of the more complex aspects of our lives would remain incomprehensible. Much as advanced statistical mechanics are necessary for designing and understanding complex physical systems, but are not readily understood by all, so the model of the *partzufim* is necessary for understanding the deeper secrets of the spiritual realm, even though they too are not readily understood.

However, there are a few points that even the beginning student of Kabbalah should be aware of. First, there are six primary *partzufim*, each composed of a binary complex of secondary *partzufim* (one male and one female), as follows:

sefirah	primary *partzuf*		secondary *partzufim*	
keter crown	עַתִּיק יוֹמִין *Atik Yomin*	The Ancient of Days	עַתִּיק יוֹמִין *Atik Yomin*	[The male facet of] the Ancient of Days
			נוּקְבֵיה דְעַתִּיק יוֹמִין *Nukvei d'Atik Yomin*	The female [facet] of the Ancient of Days
	אֲרִיךְ אַנְפִּין *Arich Anpin*	The Long Face	אֲרִיךְ אַנְפִּין *Arich Anpin*	[The male facet of] the Long Face
			נוּקְבֵיה דַאֲרִיךְ אַנְפִּין *Nukvei d'Arich Anpin*	The female [facet] of the Long Face
chochmah wisdom	אַבָּא *Abba*	Father	אַבָּא עִילָּאָה *Abba Ila'ah*	Supernal Father
			אִמָּא עִילָּאָה *Ima Ila'ah*	Supernal Mother
binah under-standing	אִמָּא *Ima*	Mother	יִשְׂרָאֵל סַבָּא *Yisrael Saba*	Israel the Elder
			תְּבוּנָה *Tevunah*	Comprehension
midot emotional and habitual *sefirot*	זְעֵיר אַנְפִּין *Z'eir Anpin*	The Small Face	יִשְׂרָאֵל *Yisrael*	Israel
			לֵאָה *Leah*	Leah
malchut kingdom	נוּקְבֵיה דִזְעֵיר אַנְפִּין *Nukvei d'Z'eir Anpin*	The Female of *Z'eir Anpin*	יַעֲקֹב *Yaakov*	Jacob
			רָחֵל *Rachel*	Rachel

As can be seen from the chart, the *partzufim* correspond to the *sefirot*, retaining the Kabbalistic dictum that regardless of the complexity of a model, it can always be expressed in terms of a more generalized, less particularized model. In this case, the more complex model of the *partzufim* (more complex, because each *partzuf* is itself made up of the full gamut of the *sefirot*, which continue to develop into a complete human-like figure containing 613 individual components) can be expressed in terms of the *sefirot*.

For example, the *sefirah* of kingdom corresponds to the primary *partzuf: Nukvei d'Zeir Anpin* (the female [facet] of The Small Face) and into the pair of secondary *partzufim* (one male and one female, both within the primary female *partzuf*) called "Jacob" and "Rachel," each of which possesses all the ten *sefirot* arranged in three axes as we saw above, 248 limbs and 365 sinews.

Notes:

1. For an in-depth discussion of this topic, see *Consciousness & Choice*, pp. 16-19.

2. See also *The Art of Education*, pp. 39ff.

3. Above we explained that foundation is the *sefirah* associated with covenants. In the *Zohar* (III, 230a), foundation (especially, its inner experiential quality of truth) and faith form a masculine/feminine pair of complementary powers, as in the liturgical phrase "truth and faith" (first benediction following the evening *Shema*; see also *Berachot* 12a). The *Zohar* also explains that there is no faith without a covenant. The numerical illustration of this is that 6 times the value of the word "faith" (אֱמוּנָה), 102, is equal to the value of "covenant" (בְּרִית), 612. The sum of the letters of the Hebrew word for "faith" written according to the Kabbalistic guidelines known as posterior and anterior (see *The Art of Education*, p. 255): א אמ אמו אמונ אמונה אמונה מונה ונה נה ה is also 612.

4. In Hebrew: הַמַּאֲמִין הָרִאשׁוֹן. The Mittler Rebbe's *Torat Chaim, Vayeira* 106d, and elsewhere.

5. For Abraham's role in establishing the faith of the Jewish soul, see *The Art of Education*, pp. 65ff.

6. This is especially true for deriving innovative Torah which originates in the soul of Moses.

7. *Ta'anit* 9a. Indeed, the first appearance of the word "manna" (*man*, in Hebrew) in the Torah is in the phrase *man hu* (מָן הוּא, literally, "what is it," or, according to some commentaries, "it is food"), which permutes into the word *emunah*, "faith" (אֱמוּנָה).

8. *Tanya*, ch. 42.

9. *Tikunei Zohar* 69 (112a, 114a).

10. In the language of Chassidut, selflessness is the ability to experience the nothingness (*ayin*) of our own being within the all-encompassing radiance of God's infinite Being (*or ein sof*).

11. The association of understanding with the maternal is illustrated in the verse: "For, if you call upon understanding..." (Proverbs 2:3). The word "if," in Hebrew (אם), can also be read as "mother" (אֵם).

12. Psalms 113:9.

13. Thus we find that many women some time after giving birth want another child, regardless of how difficult the pregnancy and labor were. The woman innately understands that the joy brought by every newborn child is an expression of the sweetening of the harsh judgments in their source (see p. 149), and feels like "an individual who has a hundred, wants two-hundred." The mixed message of satisfaction with dissatisfaction many times confuses her spouse. The dissatisfaction is caused by her feeling that she has not yet reached her final rectified state. In Kabbalah, this dissatisfaction is viewed as the reason that understanding is "expansive," forever spreading (see the correspondence of understanding with the *hei* of *Havayah* and expansion on p. 129ff.) Immediately setting her gaze on the future also saves the mother principle from experiencing her present satisfaction as her own success, disconnecting her from the Divine. A Biblical example illustrating this point is that the dough taken by the Children of Israel out of Egypt did not get a chance to rise, that is to become acidic by fermentation (Exodus 12:39; see also the Passover *Hagadah*). Though they experienced tremendous satisfaction in having surmounted Egypt, it did not show and was not to their detriment (in Hebrew, "not *get a chance* to rise" can be read "not *satisfy* to rise").

14. Genesis 2:24.

15. Ibid. 4:1.

16. See in length in *Consciousness & Choice*. The *sefirah* of knowledge is also the source of consciousness in our experience as human beings.

17. The Arizal explained the various intentions in terms of the intellect. Chassidut translates the intellectual language of the Arizal into an experiential language, thus informing the heart

(which is experiential and emotional) through the mind (which is intellectual). This in itself—the mind informing the heart—is the consummate form of unification within the individual. In fact, the area of the body associated with the *sefirah* of knowledge, the progenitor of unification, is the top-back of the neck, which lies as a link between the head (mind) and the torso (heart).

18. The Arizal also taught us to take upon ourselves the commandment of "Love your fellow as yourself" (Leviticus 19:18) before praying, implying that the purpose of the unifications created above through prayer is to create unity between our souls below. The final purpose of prayer is thus said before even beginning to pray, following the Divine rule that "the goal should be in mind form the outset" (*Lecha Dodi*, based on a similar statement in *Sefer Yetzirah* [1:7]: "the end is enwedged in the beginning").

19. In pre-Arizal Kabbalistic terminology, loving-kindness was usually called "greatness" (*gedulah*), which in Hebrew also refers to the power of growth.

20. Pre-Newtonian mechanics (and even Newton) himself, described the attraction between bodies as a state of "love." Modern physics calls this attractive force gravitation, which is still defined as an action at a distance as it requires no medium to propagate. It is in a similar sense that love has the power to span distance, and bring together even those who are far apart.

21. Deuteronomy 6:5.

22. In the original Hebrew this verse contains 39, or 3 times 13 letters. Recall that the numerical value of "love" in Hebrew (אַהֲבָה) is 13, thus the number of letters alludes to the 3 stages of "love" that the verse describes, a beautiful example of self-reference. 39 is also the value of "*God* is One" (יְ‑הוה אֶחָד), the two last words of the verse preceding this one: "Hear, O Israel: *God* is our God, *God* is one," implying that that true love for God is generated from the cognizance of God's absolute unity.

23. Alter Rebbe's *Likutei Torah, Nitzavim* 50b. See *Avodah Zarah* 3b.

24. Deuteronomy 8:18.

25. 1 Samuel 15:29.

26. Which is also the reason that the holy Name *Tzevakot* (צְבָאוֹת) was only revealed by the prophets (see p. 152ff.).

27. *Yonat Elem*, ch. 2; *Eitz Chaim* 23:1, and elsewhere.

28. The word *hod*, the Hebrew name for the *sefirah* of acknowledgment, whose inner experience is sincerity, is the etymological source for the word *yehudi*, a Jew.

29. Proverbs 10:9, and elsewhere.

30. *Shabbat* 55a.

31. Genesis 2:3.

32. Jeremiah 31:2.

33. See p. 73.

34. See *Body, Mind, and Soul*, chs. 2 and 3.

35. *Zohar* III, 233b-234a.

36. Song of Songs 2:6.

37. Introduction to *Tikunei Zohar*.

38. Ecclesiastes 8:4.

39. The first sign of sovereignty is that the king is so named. This is "his word" acting indirectly to establish his kingdom. Then the king is able to rule by speaking directly.

PART III

NAMES OF GOD

Why do Israel pray and the Almighty does not respond?
Because they do not know how to have intent on the Name! As
the verse says: "He knows My Name, he will call Me and I
shall respond."

Pesikta Rabati 22:7

IN PART III, WE WILL CONTEMPLATE THE DIFFERENT NAMES OF GOD IN Jewish tradition. The Hebrew word for "Names" is *shemot*, or in its singular form, *shem*.[1]

Names vs. *Sefirot*

Just like the *sefirot*, the Names of God reveal certain aspects of His Being. What then is the difference between a Name and a *sefirah*. For one, the Names of God are clearly mentioned in the Bible. A handwritten Torah scroll is written by a *sofer*, a scribe. Before inscribing any of the Names of God on the Torah's parchment, the *sofer* must sanctify his thoughts.[2] The names of the *sefirot*, on the other hand, when they appear in the Bible, are not treated in any special way.

Chassidic teachings add to this by explaining that the difference between God's Names and the *sefirot* can best be understood in the context of our direct relationship with the Almighty in prayer. When praying, God can only be addressed using His Names, but He cannot be addressed through the *sefirot*. Translating this difference into grammar, we would say that the Names of God are like proper nouns, while the *sefirot* are like adjectives. In the words of the sages: "we must address God and not His attributes [adjectives]."[3] In simple words, when addressing God with any one of His Names we are addressing God Himself, whereas were we to turn to Him as *the crown* or as *the wisdom* we would be addressing His attributes, which emanate from His essence but are not He Himself. While, as we shall see, there is a correspondence between the Divine Names and the *sefirot*, the Names refer to the essence of God, the Emanator, within His emanations, not to the emanations themselves.

The Arizal stressed the importance of knowing the Names of the Almighty and their meanings. In the spirit of the quote introducing this chapter, the Arizal revealed the *kavanot*—the Kabbalistic meanings and mystical intentions of the prayer service's text—as based on the holy Names of the Almighty.

As we shall see in chapter 11, the Ba'al Shem Tov stressed heartfelt devotion during prayer. Thus, the importance of knowing the Names of the Almighty and their meanings became secondary. Nonetheless, knowledge of God's Names remains essential for gaining a clear understanding of Kabbalah, especially in its contemplative and meditative forms.

Four Categories of Holy Names

In general, there are four different categories of Names ascribed to the Almighty. The first is the essential Name יהוה, also called the Tetragrammaton, meaning, *the four-letter Name*. Because of the special sanctity of the four-letter Name, it was only pronounced in the Holy Temple in Jerusalem. To refer to it, we use one of its four-letters' permutations, הֲוָיָה which is pronounced: *Havayah*.

In the second category are those Names, which by Jewish law are sacred and may not be erased. We will examine each of these Names in chapter 9.

The third category includes the connotations used to describe God in the Bible (and by the sages). The largest and most explicit group of Divine connotations that appears in the Torah is the Thirteen Principles of Divine Mercy. We will examine them and a few other connotations in chapter 10.

Finally, the fourth category of Names includes *all* the words that appear in the Torah! Kabbalah teaches us that the entire Torah is indeed one great Name of God[4] and that each of its words is a Divine Name in particular. We will examine this group of Names in chapter 11.

These four categories of Divine Names can be seen to correspond to the four letters of God's essential Name, *Havayah*, a subject we will return to at the end of chapter 11.

Notes:

1. The Hebrew word for "name" is *shem*, the given name of one of Noah's three sons (Genesis 5:32), implying that his role was the preservation and sanctification of the Divine Name. Today, the children of Shem are called Semites, where this word is usually (exclusively) identified with the Jewish people.

2. *Shulchan Aruch, Yoreh Dei'ah* 276.

3. Addressing God in prayer is considered an act of approaching God and can only be done through God's proper Names. The *sefirot* are the vehicle by which God casts His benevolence on our reality (be it physical or spiritual), in a sense, the act of God approaching reality. A similar distinction is made regarding the role of a doctor. Whereas prayers for health can be addressed only to the Almighty, the actual energy that heals may pass through a doctor. In general, the rule that God affects us through the medium of a distinct "attribute," like the *sefirot* or a righteous individual (a *tzadik*) or a doctor, leads to the conclusion that whenever we beseech God for His aid, we should make a "vessel," i.e., take action of our own accord so that God's blessing can have a place to subsist in. It is important to know that all idolatry begins with the mistake of treating the medium, the vessel, as a false "god."

4. Rabbi Moses ben Nachman (Nachmanides) in the introduction to his commentary on the Torah.

God's Essential Name   8

THE ESSENTIAL NAME OF THE ALMIGHTY, I.E., THE NAME THAT portrays His essence,[1] is spelled by the four letters יהוה. It is the most sacred of God's Names. In English, this Name is referred to as the Tetragrammaton, meaning the four-letter Name, because in Hebrew it is spelled with four letters.

God's essential Name is surely the most important word in the Torah. In the Five Books of Moses this Name appears exactly 1820 times,[2] a finding that was revealed only about 120 years ago.[3] Because of its sanctity it is never articulated. Instead it is referred to either by the word *Hashem*, which simply means "the Name," or *Havayah* (הֲוָיָה), one of the 12 possible permutations of its letters. Due to its great sanctity, this Name may only be pronounced in the Holy Temple, and its correct pronunciation is not known today.

There are many verses in the Bible in which God's essential Name appears twice or more. Sometimes, the repetition even seems redundant. The most prominent among these is the first of the two verses that contain the Thirteen Principles of Divine Mercy, which begin with the words: "*Havayah, Havayah,....*"[4] The seemingly redundant appearance of the essential Name in this verse is interpreted in Chassidic teachings as referring to two ways in which the Name describes the Almighty. One way refers to God's essence as it manifests in creation. The other way refers to His essence as it transcends creation.

We cannot grasp the meaning of the higher, transcendent level of God's essential Name, for indeed it is beyond our very conception of meaning. But the meaning of God's essential Name as manifest in creation can be understood. In fact, etymologically, the Name *Havayah* is derived from the Hebrew root הָיָה, the root form of the verb "to be." The Name's grammatical form implies "bringing into existence." Thus, God's essential Name, as manifest in creation, can be understood to mean, "He who continuously brings [all reality] into existence."[5] Accordingly, all of life and existence can be conceived of as a four-stage unfolding process that corresponds to the four letters of God's essential Name. We now proceed to look at how the Name *Havayah* reveals how God is manifest through creation.

As mentioned in chapter 4, God's essential Name is actually the most basic contemplative model in Kabbalah. In Chassidut the four stages of the creative process are known as: contraction, expansion, extension, and (second) expansion. They correspond to the letters of God's essential Name, as follows:

י (*yud*)	contraction
ה (*hei*)	expansion
ו (*vav*)	extension
ה (*hei*)	expansion

The Essential Name and the *Sefirot*

Recall that in the previous chapter we discussed the *sefirot* in the context of Divinity, by looking at God's creative act. Indeed, since the essential Name of God refers to His essence as the (continuous) Creator, it follows that the *sefirot* are a manifestation of this Name. In other words, the ten *sefirot* can be understood as an explicit revelation of the same four-stage Divine process of creation encoded in the four-letter Name.

The letter *yud* (י) is known in Kabbalah as a "formed point," meaning that though it resembles a small point, still it is well formed. The point-like nature of the *yud* graphically symbolizes the stage of contraction. Conceptually, it corresponds to the *sefirah* of wisdom, whose seminal nature is likened many times to a point of potential through which something enters reality. Wisdom serves as the entry point for intellectual energy to penetrate the mind.

The letter *hei* (ה) is drawn with three lines, which represent the expansion of the point of the *yud* into all three spatial dimensions.[6] Conceptually, it parallels the task of the *sefirah* of understanding: to expand and develop the seminal point of energy that is the *sefirah* of wisdom.

Because of their enduring partnership, wisdom and understanding are likened to a father (אַבָּא) and mother (אִמָּא). The mother, symbolized by the letter *hei*, is impregnated by the seminal point of energy given by the father. The mother encloses the father's seed of wisdom and nurtures it in her womb. The fetus of understanding grows and expands in the womb until reaching full development, ready to be born into reality.

The letter *vav* (ו) resembles a vertical line that extends downwards, connecting the higher realms with the lower. As such, it graphically symbolizes the stage of extension. The numerical value of the letter *vav* is 6 and it corresponds to the six emotive *sefirot* from loving-kindness to foundation, which are collectively known as attributes (*midot*). Building on the imagery of wisdom and understanding as father and mother, the six attributes are considered to be the sons born from the mother's womb.

The *vav*'s power of extension allows it to carry the concealed reality of understanding (the first *hei*) into the revealed reality represented by the *sefirah* of kingdom, which corresponds to the second *hei*. Like in the first *hei*, the letter's three lines represent the three spatial dimensions, but this time of our imminent and revealed reality, also known as God's kingdom on earth. In Kabbalah, the matriarch Leah who gave birth to six sons and one daughter represents the mother figure. Conceptually, the second *hei* is likened to the daughter of the family.

We have covered 9 out of the 10 *sefirot*. What is missing is the *sefirah* of crown. As was stressed in the previous chapters, crown represents those things, like the super-conscious, that are transcendent or anterior to our perceptible reality. Indeed, though there is no letter that represents the *sefirah* of crown directly, it is (appropriately) merely alluded to by the upper tip of the first letter, the *yud*. In Kabbalah, the *yud*'s upper tip is called the "formless point," i.e., a simple point possessing no spatial dimensions, a name that indicates the unfathomable transcendence of the crown, to which it refers. As the *yud* and the first *hei* are the father and mother, the upper tip of the *yud* points to the third partner[7] in marriage: God, from Whom the infinite power to procreate derives.

The full correspondence of the letters of God's essential Name to the *sefirot* is as follows:

קוצו של י (tip of *yud*)	crown	God
י (*yud*)	wisdom	father
ה (*hei*)	understanding	mother
ו (*vav*)	loving-kindness thru foundation	sons
ה (*hei*)	kingdom	daughter

The Essential Name and the Human Body

Above, we saw how the *sefirot* correspond to the parts of the human body. Let us now examine how the letters of the essential Name of God correspond in a similar fashion.

In Ezekiel's vision of the resurrection of the dead,[8] we find a four-level depiction of the body as it is reconstituted—bones, blood vessels, flesh, and skin. The fifth level, the spirit, which Ezekiel prophesizes about separately, gives life to the inanimate body.

The bones, blood vessels, flesh, and skin correspond to the four letters of the Divine Name, with the tip of the *yud* corresponding to the fifth transcendent (and categorically different) level of the spirit as follows:

קוצו של י (tip of *yud*)	crown	spirit of life
י (*yud*)	wisdom	bones
ה (*hei*)	understanding	blood vessels
ו (*vav*)	loving-kindness thru foundation	flesh
ה (*hei*)	kingdom	skin

Let us explain this chart in some detail. The first letter of the Divine Name, *yud* (י), is the most compact of all the Hebrew letters, serving in a sense as their structural core. In the human body the *yud* therefore corresponds to the bones and the skeletal frame in general. The skeletal system, the core frame of the human body, supports all the other physiological systems, the muscular system, the circulatory system, the nervous system, etc., which are layered upon it.[9]

In addition, the *yud* often symbolizes a seed, from which new life emerges. As such, it corresponds to the bone marrow, which produces blood cells (which constitute three fourths of the body's cells).

The second letter of the Divine Name, *hei* (ה), refers to the *sefirah* of understanding as it resides in the heart and from there spreads out to enliven and animate the entire body and its organs. As a physiological system, the *hei* corresponds to the circulatory system—the body's inner channel of life force, its most basic level of self-consciousness and self-preservation. The *hei* expands in all three dimensions from the seminal point of the *yud*, the bone marrow.

The third letter of the Divine Name, *vav*, refers to the six emotive attributes, as noted above. Emotive attributes are to the *sefirah* of understanding (the first *hei*) as the flesh that fills out the body is to the blood vessels that it enclothes. Rectified emotions are referred to in the Bible as "the heart of flesh."[10] Thus, the *vav* of God's essential Name corresponds to the flesh that Ezekiel saw in his prophecy.

The fourth letter of the Divine Name, the final *hei*, refers to the skin, the most exterior layer, which serves as the body's clothing. Skin serves as well as the body's sensor and protector and is responsible for its appearance, thus fittingly serving as the kingdom (*malchut*) of the four general divisions of the body.

Whenever the four-level model of God's essential Name *Havayah* is used to contemplate existence, there is always a fifth, higher and all-inclusive level that resides above the four to enliven them. The fifth level corresponds to the upper tip of the *yud* of God's Name. This fifth level is the spiritual source of existence, the spirit of life, as drawn into the body by means of the respiratory system.

The Essential Name and the Four Worlds

Just as the letters of *Havayah* reveal the structure of the *sefirot* and the body, they also correspond to the model of the four worlds: Emanation, Creation, Formation, and Action (commonly denoted by an acronym comprising their initial letters in Hebrew: *Abya*). Though usually the word "world" strikes up images of physical space and the objects and creatures that inhabit that space, in Kabbalah, worlds refers, first and foremost, to states of consciousness. Entering a world means entering a certain conscious state or perspective on one's own being and surroundings.

Kabbalah divides the infinitude of possible perspectives on reality into four general categories. The differential characteristic distinguishing between the Four Worlds is the amount of selflessness, or nullification of self in each.

In the highest world, the World of Emanation, selflessness is so powerful that independent selfhood cannot even be imagined. The World of Emanation is described as being absolutely one with the Creator, which leaves no possibility for a reality distinct from Him. The *Tikunei Zohar* describes this state of being as "He and His Life are one, He and His Self are one,"[11] where "His Life" refers to the lights of the *sefirot* of the World of Emanation, and "His Self" refers to the vessels of its *sefirot*.

In the World of Creation, selfhood can be imagined, but consciousness is not yet independent enough of the Creator to be considered fully distinct. In this world, independent reality exists only as a possibility.

The World of Formation is where perspective is based on generalities; particulars are not yet possible at this level of consciousness. In Formation there is already a sense of selfhood, but only when grasped in language that is not personal. What this means is that though there can be consciousness of Lion as a type of animal, consciousnesness can not yet differentiate between particular, real lions. Regarding one's self, one can be aware of the existence of humanity, or even of a particular nation, but not of one's own self as part of humanity or that nation.

Finally, the consciousness of the World of Action grants the perspective that we are usually accustomed to regarding our selves. Here consciousness is able to grasp itself as a distinct and separate entity with its own being.

The Four Worlds correspond to the letters of *Havayah* as follows:

' (*yud*)	Emanation	אֲצִילוּת
ה (*hei*)	Creation	בְּרִיאָה
ו (*vav*)	Formation	יְצִירָה
ה (*hei*)	Action	עֲשִׂיָּה

To deepen our understanding of the Worlds and to begin to see how the templates of Kabbalah exist in parallel and divulge layer upon layer of meaning, let us see how the Worlds correspond to the *sefirot*. To prevent confusion we must stress again that everything in Kabbalah is essentially holographic. Meaning, that though each world contains within itself all of the *sefirot* (lights and vessels, as noted above regarding the World of Emanation), the Four Worlds themselves can be seen to correspond to the *sefirot* as follows:

' (*yud*)	Emanation	wisdom
ה (*hei*)	Creation	understanding
ו (*vav*)	Formation	loving-kindness thru foundation
ה (*hei*)	Action	kingdom

From this last more complex correspondence we can learn a great deal. Using the symbolic imagery of the *sefirot* as father, mother, sons, and daughter discussed above, in *Tikunei Zohar* the World of Emanation is described as the dwelling place of the father principle, and the Throne (a symbol for the World of Creation) is described as the place where the mother principle dwells. The Throne as a symbol for the World of Creation is meant to depict the descent of consciousness, for when sitting down, the head is lowered and brought closer to the feet. This state thus represents lower consciousness which already allows for the possibility of being that is (only seemingly) separate and distinct from the Creator. Kabbalah locates the source of souls as "beneath the Throne,"[12] implying that though souls originate in the World of Creation, they possess an innate ability to descend such that their consciousness grasps the reality of the lower Worlds.

Above we mentioned that the father and mother principles are always united, never fully severing their bond. As such, though the Throne is a symbol for the World of Creation (which corresponds to the mother principle) its awning represents the consciousness of the father principle, the World of Emanation, which is forever hovering close to the mother.

In Chassidut, the image of the Throne and the act of sitting as metapohors for the *sefirah* of understanding are explained in depth. Sitting is comparable to the intellectual act of understanding, an idea captured in the Hebrew idiom "the sitting [i.e., stability] of consciousness" (יִשׁוּב הַדַּעַת)[13]; in English, similar usage is made in the idiom "this dish does not sit well with me," meaning that it is not well digested. To have a real and lasting effect, knowledge must be internalized, indicating that true understanding is related to internalization and assimilation.[14] Since the World of Creation is the origin of souls, we learn that the soul can be reached primarily through understanding.

Below the origin of the souls in the World of Creation is the World of Formation, the origin of the angels. As noted, the World of Formation corresponds to the emotional and habitual realm of the *sefirot*: loving-kindness through foundation. That is why the archangels are usually identified with these *sefirot*: Michael corresponds to loving-kindness, Gabriel to might, Rephael to Beauty, etc.

Finally, the lowest World, the World of Action, which corresponds to the *sefirah* of kingdom, serves as the origin of the forces and laws of natural motion. In the vision of Ezekiel, natural motion is described as governed by the *Ofanim*, angels that move by rotating, much like a bicycle wheel. Kabbalah explains that motion and force in nature are circular as they lack free will which would free them from their repetitive cyclical nature. Thus, the consciousness of the World of Action generates an astounding paradox: on the one hand, it grants those who have it a feeling of being independent and separate from the Almighty, on the other, it precludes true free will, locking one in one's own repetitive and incorrigible being. It is only by tapping into higher levels of consciousness that we are able to, in any way, break the mold of our own selves. Many of the Torah's commandments focus on rectifying the World of Action,[15] which is why many of them are prescribed daily. Of all the commandments, daily prayer is the most illustrative of our focus on the *sefirah* of kingdom and the World of Action. By repeating the same prayers day after day, we sustain the consciousness of the World of Action and reconnect it with the higher worlds, making sure that it does not fall into a state of total separation from the higher spiritual realms. Just as the performance of recurring daily chores like eating, drinking, sleeping, etc., sustain life, prayer (and other commandments focused on the World of Action) sustain free will and our ability to continually develop spiritually.

To gain a clearer understanding of the different levels of consciousness inherent in each of the Four Worlds, we will make one final correspondence, reflecting upon the image of the rectified individual that inhabits each. A mistake that is commonly made before studying Chassidut is that Kabbalah prescribes that every person should attain the consciousness of the highest world, the World of Emanation. Chassidut teaches us that in reality, by nature, not everyone is capable of doing so. In fact, the overwhelming majority of people cannot.[16] Instead, as each of the Four Worlds is actually a composite of all four (we have referred to this as the inter-inclusive, or holographic nature of Kabbalistic models), our real goal is to attain the level of Emanation within the level of consciousness suited to us.

Individuals possessing the consciousness of the World of Emanation are unique and rare. They are called *tzadikim* and the Bible describes them as "the foundation of the world."[17] The Almighty places them in each generation to guide others by lighting their environs with the energy of holiness and Divinity.[18]

Inhabiting the World of Creation is the scholar of the Torah whose entire being is focused on mastering the complexities of the revealed dimension of the Torah, the Talmud and *Halachah*, together with the secrets of the concealed dimension. The Torah scholar is described in Hebrew as "one who knows the Book,"[19] referring to the Torah. The consciousness of the World of Creation already offers the Torah scholar a certain sense of separate and independent being from the Almighty, which can lead to feelings of superiority over less scholarly individuals. The rectified Torah scholar though, as taught by the Ba'al Shem Tov, taps into the level of Emanation that is included within the World of Creation and feels that as much as he has learnt and understood, the Torah still lies pure and whole before him, untouched and untasted. Thus, in his inner being he experiences the Torah's everlasting freshness as the Almighty continues to delight in it as His object of recreation.[20]

The consciousness of the World of Formation corresponds to the emotional realm of the soul from loving-kindness to foundation, and the individual with a rectified Formation consciousness is referred to as a joyful *chasid*. Joy permeates the heart (as it is said: "You have given joy into my heart"[21]) from its origin in the *sefirah* of understanding, the mother of all the heart's emotions. Indeed, joy unites all of the emotive attributes of the heart, even the apparent opposites of love and fear.[22] In addition, joy combats and counterbalances the sorrow of the heart brought about by self-consciousness. To unite opposites and counterbalance self-consciousness are expressions of Emanation drawn into the consciousness of the World of Formation by the attribute of joy. Thus, the joyful *chasid* (the literal meaning of *chasid* is a man of loving-kindness, *chesed*, the primary attribute of the heart) is characteristic of the rectified state of the heart in the World of Formation.

Finally, the great majority of consciousness lies in the World of Action. The rectified individual in this realm is described as the "simple Jew." Years ago this term was used to describe uneducated Jews who could just barely read prayers in Hebrew. In Chassidut though it refers to any Jew who for all of his sophistication and complexity (he can even be a great scholar) is dedicated to the tasks of life and the Torah in a simple, honest, and unassuming manner. The simple, pure faith in God of a simple Jew is the manifestation of Emanation in the World of Action. In Hebrew, simplicity also stems from the word meaning "[fully] exposed," implying that ultimately the highest nature of the Almighty (even above the revelation of Divinity in the World of Emanation), when exposed, will be revealed in the consciousness of the World of Action and the simple Jews that inhabit it.

As noted, each of these four types of individuals reflects the level of Emanation within each of the Four Worlds. Indeed, numerically, the four idioms used to describe them, in Hebrew, are exactly equal to one another:

"The *tzadik* the foundation of the world" (צַדִּיק יְסוֹד עוֹלָם) = "One who knows the Book" (יוֹדֵעַ סֵפֶר) = "A joyful *chasid*" (חָסִיד שָׂמֵחַ) = "A simple Jew" (יְהוּדִי פָּשׁוּט) = 430. 430 is the numerical value of the word "soul" (נֶפֶשׁ), implying that every soul possesses the potential to become one of these four, depending upon the soul's root in one of the four spiritual worlds, and moreover, that each and every soul is gifted with an innate affinity to each of the four spiritual archtypes.

Havayah: the Soul of the *Sefirot*

Each of the *sefirot* is a composite of Divine light within a vessel. The Divine light enters the vessel of the *sefirah* much as the soul enters the body in order to enliven it. For each *sefirah*, the particular aspect of the Divine light that enters it corresponds to a particular meditative vocalization of the essential Name, *Havayah*. The vessel of each *sefirah* corresponds to one of the sanctified Names of God that belong to the second category of Names, which will be discussed in the next chapter. Thus, each of the *sefirot* is actually a composite of a form of the essential Name of the Almighty as it enlivens one of His other sanctified Names. In the World of Emanation, where these Names are principally manifested, both the vessels and the lights of the *sefirot* are manifestations of Divinity. At consciousness levels lower than Emanation, the lights represent the Divine essence that is enclothed within the mundane aspects of reality.

Each of the meditative vocalizations of the essential Name, *Havayah*, is formed by using one of the Hebrew vowel signs together with each of the four letters of the Name. It should be noted that all of these vocalizations are mystical in nature and do not appear anywhere in the Bible. They are never pronounced because, as mentioned, it is forbidden to pronounce the Name *Havayah* with any vocalization. Instead, the vocalizations are used as the subject of deep meditation during prayer.

The order of the vocalizations as they signify the lights of the *sefirot* is as follows:

crown כתר

יְהֹוָה

understanding בינה

יְהֹוָה

wisdom חכמה

יְהֹוָה

might גבורה

יִהֹוָה

loving-kindness חסד

יְהֹוָה

beauty תפארת

יֱהֹוֶה

acknowledgment הוד

יְהֶוָה

victory נצח

יְהֹוָה

foundation יסוד

יְרְהֹוָוּהוּ

kingdom מלכות

יהוה

Notice that the *sefirah* of kingdom's *Havayah* is without a vowel sign altogether. This is because kingdom possesses nothing of its own, but rather receives all of its Divine energy from the *sefirot* that precede it.

Apart from these nine meditative vocalizations of the essential Name *Havayah*, there are two other vocalizations that appear explicitly in the Torah. The first and most common vocalization (close to all 1820 instances of *Havayah* in the Five Books of Moses) is the letters of *Havayah* with the vowel signs of the holy Name אֲדֹנָי (when this Name appears outside of the Bible or the liturgy, it is customarily pronounced "*Adni*"). The Name is then written יֱהֹוִה and in sacred contexts is pronounced as אֲדֹנָי. In non-sacred contexts it is usually referred to as simply *Hashem* (the Name) or *Havayah*. Kabbalistically, this is the primary manifestation of the Name *Havayah* and relates in particular to the vessel of the *sefirah* of beauty (to be discussed in the next chapter), whose inner experience is mercy. Therefore, throughout the Torah, God's essential Name *Havayah* is associated with the principle of mercy, the fundamental manner in which God relates to creation. This is the reason that, in the Talmud, the sages refer to the Almighty as "the Merciful One" (*Rachmana*), as noted above.

The second explicit vocalization of *Havayah* in the Torah is with the vowel signs of the Name *Elokim* (יֱהֹוִה),[23] and is pronounced "*Elokim*." This vocalization corresponds to the vessel of the *sefirah* of understanding and we will discuss it further in the next chapter.

Letter Fillings of the Essential Name

One of the most important concepts in Kabbalah is that of *letter filling*. This refers to writing out a letter as it would be vocalized. For instance, the first letter of the Hebrew alphabet, *alef* (א) would be written out as the three letters *alef lamed pei* (אָלֶף). The initial letter of the letter filling is naturally the letter itself, or the root letter, while the newly revealed additional letters are considered the filling letters.

Letter filling reveals the hidden potential inherent within each of the 22 letters of the Hebrew alphabet, as it creates a bridge between the letter in its written form and the letter when it is vocalized in speech (thus symbolizing the unity of the Written Torah and the Oral Tradition). In the language of Kabbalah, every letter is pregnant with its filling and writing out the filling is like opening the womb of the letter.

The holiest and most important word in the Torah is of course God's essential Name, *Havayah*, the source of all else. As such, much of the Arizal's Kabbalah is based on the letter filling of this Name. In fact, the letter filling of *Havayah* makes its appearance in the Arizal's cosmogony (i.e., the order of creation) long before the *sefirot* become revealed. Indeed, in the *kavanot*, the mystical intentions taught by the Arizal, the filling of *Havayah* is key.

A few of the Hebrew letters can be filled in more than one way. In the Name *Havayah*, spelled *yud* (י) *hei* (ה) *vav* (ו) *hei* (ה), the letters *hei* (ה) and *vav* (ו) can be filled in the following ways:

ה can be filled as הי, הא, or הה

ו can be filled as וי, ואו, or וו

Some quick math will tell us that because of these variations, *Havayah* can be filled in 27 different ways,[24] as follows:

ה	ו	ה	י	numerical value
הי	ויו	הי	יוד	72
אה	ויו	הי	יוד	63
הה	ויו	הי	יוד	67
הי	ואו	הי	יוד	63
אה	ואו	הי	יוד	54
הה	ואו	הי	יוד	58
הי	וו	הי	יוד	62
אה	וו	הי	יוד	53
הה	וו	הי	יוד	57
הי	ויו	הא	יוד	63
אה	ויו	הא	יוד	54
הה	ויו	הא	יוד	58
הי	ואו	הא	יוד	54
אה	ואו	הא	יוד	45
הה	ואו	הא	יוד	49
הי	וו	הא	יוד	53
אה	וו	הא	יוד	44
הה	וו	הא	יוד	48
הי	ויו	הה	יוד	67
אה	ויו	הה	יוד	58
הה	ויו	הה	יוד	62
הי	ואו	הה	יוד	53
אה	ואו	הה	יוד	58
הה	ואו	הה	יוד	49
הי	וו	הה	יוד	57
אה	וו	הה	יוד	48
הה	וו	הה	יוד	52

The sum of the numerical values of all 27 fillings is 1521. In a beautiful example of self-reference, 1521 is also the square of 39, which is the numerical value of the phrase *"Havayah [is] One"* (יְ־הוה אֶחָד)!

The sum of the root letters, meaning the initial letters of each filling, is of course 27 · 26 = 702, the numerical value of "Shabbat" (שַׁבָּת). And, the sum of the filling letters is 819, which is the sum of the squares of the integers from 1 to 13 (i.e., 1+4+9+16+..+169 = 819). 819 is the numerical value of the Hebrew idiom אַחְדוּת פְּשׁוּטָה, which means "absolute Oneness," an idiom commonly appearing in Chassidut to describe the Oneness of *Havayah*. Indeed, in mathematical language, 819 is referred to as the pyramid of 13, 13 being the numerical value of the word "one" (אֶחָד), in Hebrew.

Of these 27 possible fillings of *Havayah*, the *Zohar* and the Arizal identify four as most central:

ה	ו	ה	י	
הי	וי	הי	יוד	72
הי	ואו	הי	יוד	63
הא	ואו	הא	יוד	45
הה	וו	הה	יוד	52

These four central fillings are referred to by their numerical values, in Kabbalah. In another example of the holographic quality of Kabbalistic models, these fillings also form a four-tiered model themselves, with each one corresponding to one of the four letters of *Havayah*: 72 corresponds to the *yud*, 63 to the first *hei*, 45 to the *vav*, and 52 to the second *hei*.

Altogether the central fillings have 39 letters, which we recall is the value of the phrase "*Havayah* [is] One" and the root of 1521, the sum of all 27 letter fillings. The sum of the central fillings' numerical values is 232, or 4 times 58; 58 is the numerical value of the Hebrew word for "grace" (חֵן).[25] In another example of self-reference, the sum of the letter fillings that make up the right to left diagonal of the chart above is 58!

Notes:

1. Although no name can fully express God's essence, the Name *Havayah refers* to God's essence. It is thus referred to as "the essential Name" (שֵׁם הָעֶצֶם), or "the unique Name" (שֵׁם הַמְיֻחָד), or and "the explicit Name" (שֵׁם הַמְפֹרָשׁ).

2. 1820 = 26 · 70. 26 is the numerical value of God's essential Name, *Havayah* (יהוה), itself. 70 is the numerical value of the word for "secret" (סוֹד), in Hebrew. Together, these two words appear in a verse regarding the importance of God's essential Name: "The secret of *Havayah* is [revealed] to those who fear Him" (סוֹד יְהוָה לִירֵאָיו), Psalms 25:14.

3. By Rabbi Pinchas Horowitz, the author of a beautiful volume on various mathematical properties of the Torah, titled *Ahavat Torah*, which means "Love of the Torah." Indeed, before the advent of computers, counting the number of times that a word appears in the Torah was a labor of love. The sages relate that title "scribe" (סוֹפֵר), like Ezra the Scribe (see Nechemiah 12:26, 36), was given on account of the person being adept at counting the letters of the Torah (see also the previous chapter regarding the relationship between "scribe" and "number," in Hebrew).

4. Exodus 34:6.

5. *Sha'ar HaYichud VeHaEmunah*, Chapter 4.

6. The letter *hei* is regarded in Kabbalah as representing a three dimensional figure projected on a two-dimensional surface. Its two longer sides (the vertical and horizontal lines that are connected) lie in the same plane, and are its width and length. The short, detached foot on its left suggests a third dimension running "into" the page as it were. Chassidic teachings explain that the letter *hei's* width, length, and depth dimensions correspond to the three means of expression (also called the three garments of the soul): thought, speech, and action. For more, see *The Hebrew Letters*, pp. 80ff.

7. *Kidushin* 30b.

8. Ezekiel 37:1-14.

9. The word for "bone" (*etzem*), in Hebrew, also means "self" or "essence," that is, the core of one's being, thus providing a spiritual correspondence between the *yud*, the essential letter in the essential Name, and the bones of the human body.

10. Ezekiel 11:19, 36:26.

11. Introduction to *Tikunei Zohar*. See *Tanya, Igeret Hakodesh* 20.

12. *Zohar* III, 29b and 123b.

13. See *Consciousness & Choice*, pp. 28-30. The morning prayer service is actually a tour of consciousness, leading the person praying through all four worlds. When reciting the *Shema*, we are in the World of Creation, which is one reason why we are normally instructed to sit while reciting it. In addition, the *Shema* itself begins with the word "hear," which as explained elsewhere is the

physical sense associated with the *sefirah* of understanding and the soul's capacity to internalize a message.

14. See also *The Art of Education*, especially chapter 1.

15. In our own generation, the Lubavitcher Rebbe stressed that "action [i.e., a consciousness focused on the World of Action and its perfection] is the main thing."

16. In explaining this, the Ba'al Shem Tov quoted the Talmud which says that "many tried to attain the level of Rabbi Shimon bar Yochai—but failed!" (*Berachot* 35b). The Ba'al Shem Tov explained that not only did they fail to attain the higher level that was not suited for them, but that by disregarding their real place and locus of rectification, they lost their own pre-destined share in the world (*Keter Shem Tov*, 4).

17. Proverbs 10:25.

18. *Yoma* 38b.

19. Isaiah 29:11.

20. God's recreational attitude towards the Torah is described as the "delights of the King in Himself."

21. Psalms 4:8.

22. In the benediction before the *Shema* we say: "And unite our heart to love and to fear Your Name." The word "unite" also means "make joyful," indicating this same idea that joy is the source of love and fear and the power to unify them.

23. For example, see Deuteronomy 3:24.

24. Note that out of the 27 values, there are only 13 unique ones and there sum is 724. The sum of the 4 most important fillings, 72, 63, 45, and 52 is 232. The sum of all 27 possible fillings is 1521. The filling that equals 45 is considered the one that acts to rectify reality, and is therefore called the Path of Emanation (*orach atzilut*). Together, $4 + 232 + 724 + 1521 = 2522$, which is equal to $97 \cdot 26$. 26 is of course the value of *Havayah*, while 97 is the sum of the two fillings 45 (מה) and 52 (בן), which are the central figures in the process of the rectification of the universe. This is another beautiful example of self-reference.

25. See in length in *The Art of Education*, Supplementary Essay G.

The Sanctified Names 9

WE NOW TURN TO LOOK AT THE SECOND CATEGORY OF GOD'S NAMES. These Names are sanctified in Jewish law, which limits their pronunciation and prohibits erasing them, or even one of their letters (or treating them with disrespect), once they have been written down.[1] In Kabbalah, each Name of God is seen to manifest the Divine power inherent in one of the *sefirot*. Thus, each of the *sefirot* has a Name that corresponds to it in particular.

אֶהְיֶה אֲשֶׁר אֶהְיֶה • pronounced *Ekyeh Asher Ekyeh*

Just as the Name *Havayah* derives from the Hebrew root "to be," so does this Name. Literally, the Name *Ekyeh* means "I will be." Unlike the Name *Havayah*, which never appears in the Bible explicitly as a verb form ("he shall bring into being") *Ekyeh* (or, when not a Name of God, pronounced *eheyeh*) appears frequently in the Bible as a verb in its literal sense of "I will be." In fact, in the entire Bible, it appears only three times in reference to the Almighty, all three in one verse during God's dialogue with Moses at the Burning Bush. There, God charged Moses with the mission of redeeming the Jewish people from Egypt:

> And Moses said to God: "Behold, when I come to the people of Israel, and shall say to them, 'The God of your fathers has sent me to you,' and they shall say to me, 'What is His Name,' what shall I say to them?"
> And God said to Moses: "*I will be* that which *I will be*," and He said, "Thus shall you say to the people of Israel, '*I will be* has sent me to you.'"[2]

As a Name of God, *Ekyeh* retains its literal meaning of "I will be," implying new birth or revelation of self. The above quote says that the essence of God's Self, as it were, will be revealed with the spiritual birth of the Jewish people through their redemption from exile.

Thus, there is a double revelation occurring. At one and the same time, the Jewish people are born into the world, while at the same time, God becomes manifest in reality through their birth. These simultaneous revelations are alluded to in the phrase: "*I will be* that which *I will be*." The first "*I will be*" reflects God's manifestation, while the second refers to the birth of the souls of Israel from the supernal womb. According to this interpretation, "*I will be* that which *I will be*" reads, I will be revealed in the world by means of the birth of My people Israel into the world, i.e., their redemption from Egypt—for My very essence is identified with My children's essence and their birth is My birth.

Ekyeh as God's manifestation of His Self corresponds to the *sefirah* of crown. *Ekyeh* as the supernal womb from which the souls of Israel are born corresponds to the *sefirah* of understanding, which, as noted, is known as the mother. It follows then that the Hebrew word אֲשֶׁר, meaning "that which," that links the two Names אהיה in this phrase corresponds to the *sefirah* of wisdom. We then have the following correspondence for the first three *sefirot*:

כֶּתֶר crown

"I will be" - אהיה

בִּינָה understanding	חָכְמָה wisdom
"I will be" – אהיה	"that which" - אֲשֶׁר

More precisely, the Name *Ekyeh* in both of its manifestations corresponds to the *sefirah* of crown. The first *Ekyeh* refers to the super-conscious aspect of the crown, that which is *yet* to be revealed. The second *Ekyeh* refers to the preconscious aspect of the crown, that which is *about* to be revealed. In the terminology of Kabbalah, the full Name "*I will be* that which *I will be*" is the origin of the first three *sefirot*—crown, wisdom, and understanding—in the *sefirah* of crown itself.

From their origin in the super-conscious crown, the two conscious *sefirot* of wisdom and understanding appear. The vessels of wisdom and understanding are associated with two other sanctified Names: wisdom with the Name *Kah* and understanding with the variant vocalization of *Havayah* as *Elokim* mentioned in the previous chapter. Let us look at these two Names.

יָהּ • pronouced *Kah*

This Name is composed of the first two letters יה of the essential Name *Havayah*, and appears twice in the Five Books of Moses[3] and many times throughout the rest of the Bible. It signifies the Divine essence of the *sefirah* of wisdom. In the Name *Havayah*, the first two letters, as explained above, correspond to the two *sefirot* of wisdom and understanding. In the holy Name *Kah*, these two letters represent the *sefirot* of wisdom and understanding as they are reflected in the *sefirah* of wisdom itself.

Because this holy Name is essentially a fragment (two letters out) of the complete (four-letter) Name *Havayah*,[4] to better understand what it represents, we need to see how the first two letters of *Havayah* (יה) relate to its last two (וה). The first two letters correspond to the concealed dimension of the Name *Havayah*, while the last two letters correspond to its revealed dimension.[5] Specifically, the first two letters refer to a concealed form of God's Providence, while the last two refer to its revealed nature. In the *Tanya*, Rabbi Shneur Zalman of Liadi develops this notion further explaining that the concealed nature of Divine Providence corresponding to the first two letters of the Name *Havayah* results from its being unfathomable to the human mind. In truth, even this concealed Divine Providence is good in its essence, but the good is too great to be grasped by our limited understanding and is therefore mistaken for bad. Nonetheless, we are taught that through the sincere expression of praise, one brings out the praiseworthy attribute in the one praised. Thus, by continually praising *Kah*, the source of God's concealed Providence, we merit to reveal and experience the infinite good and pleasure hidden in apparent suffering and thereby to transform the pain itself into pleasure and to heal the affliction.

The Book of Psalms, more than any other book in the Bible, praises the Almighty through his holy Name, *Kah*. Famous from Psalms is the expression: *Hallelu-Kah*, which means "praise *Kah*." In fact, the conclusion of the entire Book of Psalms is the verse: "Every soul shall praise *Kah*, *Hallelu-Kah*." The sages explain that the Hebrew word meaning "[every] soul" (הַנְּשָׁמָה) in this verse can also be rendered so as to mean "[every] breath" (הַנְּשִׁימָה), implying that ideally, each and every breath of life should be imbued with a conscious praise of God.[6] Then, even the apparent suffering one experiences in life can suddenly be revealed as God's overwhelming goodness.

יֱהֹוִה • pronounced *Elokim*

We already had a short encounter with this Name in the previous chapter. It is a vocalization of *Havayah* with the vowel signs of the Name *Elokim* (in Hebrew: *Havayah benikud Elokim*). It represents the manner in which the relatively masculine loving-kindness inherent in the Name *Havayah* sweetens the relatively feminine harshness represented by the Name *Elokim*. This sweetening process takes place within the feminine *sefirah* of understanding, the higher mother principle.

Sweetening the harsh judgmental character of the *sefirah* of understanding is considered the complementary task to the clarification and elevation of the fallen sparks.[7] While elevation of the sparks concentrates on the fallen energy in the mundane, the sweetening of the harsh judgments concentrates on constricted states of consciousness that prevent a balanced and inclusive understanding of the opposing forces that make up our mundane reality. In a sense, sweetening the harsh judgments is akin to expanding one's consciousness so that it can bear the fallen state of reality.[8]

This Name also alludes to contemplative meditation (*hitbonenut*, in Hebrew), which is the primary method for sweetening the harsh judgments of understanding and expanding consciousness. Contemplative meditation is symbolized in Chassidut by a goblet full of wine (כּוֹס יַיִן), the goblet symbolizing the mind and the wine symbolizing the topic of meditation. The numerical value of the word "goblet" (כּוֹס), in Hebrew, is 86, the same as the numerical value of Name *Elokim* (אֱלֹהִים). The numerical value of the Hebrew word for "wine" (יַיִן) equals 70, the same value as the sum of this Name's vowel signs.[9]

אהוה • pronounced *Akvah*

This Name is often referred to as "the goodly Name of God," because its numerical value, 17, is equal to that of the Hebrew word for "good" (טוֹב). It represents the primordial light of the first day of creation that God saw to be good[10] and then concealed; this light will only be revealed to the world in the future.[11]

Like the concealed primordial light that it represents, this Name of God is hidden and does not explicitly appear in the Bible. But, it appears implicitly. Its four letters are encoded in many Biblical phrases. The first, and most fundamental instance is in the very first verse of the Torah, "In the beginning, God created the heavens and the earth."[12] In this verse, the holy Name אהוה is encoded as the initial letters of the four words "the heavens and the earth," אֵת הַשָּׁמַיִם וְאֵת הָאָרֶץ. The encoding of *Akvah*[13] in this phrase reveals that God's purpose in creation is to manifest His infinite Divine goodness throughout reality, particularly, by unifying the two realms of "the heavens" and "the earth," i.e., the spiritual and the physical realms.

Because it signifies the Divine power to unite spirituality (heavens) and physicality (earth), this Divine Name is associated with the *sefirah* of knowledge. Knowledge is the hidden unifying force within the ten *sefirot*, just as the Name *Akvah* is hidden throughout the Torah, creating unifications throughout its text.[14]

In the Bible, the power to unify—to bind two things together—is described as "good."[15] Thus, in Kabbalah, the Name *Akvah* is related in particular to the origin of loving-kindness in the *sefirah* of knowledge, the concentrated power of the mind (knowledge) to elicit love in the heart (loving-kindness).

In Chassidut, this Name plays a special role. The name of the founder of Chassidut, the Ba'al Shem Tov, literally means "The Master of the goodly Name," specifically referring to the Name *Akvah*, "the goodly Name." The Ba'al Shem Tov's soul came to the world to reveal the Divine power of this Name. He taught that the soul of Israel possesses the ability to be in heaven (in Yiddish, *ois velt*, literally, "out of the world") and on earth (*in velt*, "in the world") simultaneously, thus serving as the Divine bridge to draw down the light of heaven to shine on earth, and thereby to fulfill Isaiah's words to be "a light unto the nations."[16]

אֵל · pronouced *Kail*

Like the Name *Kah*, the two letters that make up this Name of the Almighty, *alef* (א) and *lamed* (ל), are the first two letters of another Name, *Elokim*. Literally, as a Hebrew root, this Name means power. In Kabbalah, this Name is associated with the *sefirah* of loving-kindness, as in the verse, "The loving-kindness of *Kail* is [manifest] all day."[17] Thus, *Kail* signifies God's creative power, His unfaltering commitment to continually recreate and sustain the world through loving-kindness, as we learn from the Bible that "The world is built through loving-kindness."[18]

אֱלֹלִים · pronounced *Elokim*

This Name generally signifies the Divine attribute of judgment inherent in the *sefirah* of might. In the Bible, the same word, in a non-sacred context, means an angel[19] or a judge.[20] In Kabbalah, the Divine court, where man is judged for his deeds on earth, is located in the spiritual chamber (*heichal*) of the *sefirah* of might.

Though its main association is with the *sefirah* of might, this Name also manifests in two[21] other *sefirot*: understanding and kingdom.[22] In understanding—in addition to *Havayah* vocalized as *Elokim*—the Almighty, as the source of all life force, is called the living God (*Elokim Chayim*). As relating to kingdom, God manifests through this Name as the inner essence of nature and its laws; the numerical value of *Elokim* and the numerical value of "nature" (הַטֶּבַע) in Hebrew, both being 86, as noted above.

יְהֹוָה · pronounced *Adni*

As already explained in the previous chapter, the common form (vocalization) of the Name *Havayah* is manifest as the vessel of the *sefirah* of beauty, the embodiment of the Divine attribute of mercy.[23]

צְבָאוֹת · pronounced *Tzevakot*

As a word, *tzeva'ot* means "hosts" or "armies," and corresponds to the Divine power inherent in the *sefirot* of victory and acknowledgment. Through its means the forces of good are victorious in their war against the forces of evil, causing the evil itself to surrender to the good, i.e., to acknowledge the superiority and authority of the good.

The Name *Tzevakot* always appears following another Name. When it follows the Name *Havayah*, the combined Name refers, in particular, to the *sefirah* of victory. When it follows *Elokim*, the combined Name refers to the *sefirah* of acknowledgment.

Tzevakot does not appear in the Five Books of Moses as a Name of God; its first appearance as a holy Name is in the beginning of the Book of Samuel[24] when Chanah, Samuel's mother, beseeches God to give her a child:

> And she [Chanah] vowed a vow, and said, "O God of Hosts [*Havayah Tzevakot*], if you will indeed look on the affliction of your maidservant, and remember me, and not forget your maidservant, but will give to your maidservant a male child,

then I will give him to God all the days of his life, and no razor shall come upon his head."

God answered her prayer and gave her a son, who became the Prophet Samuel and who was "weighed as equal to Moses and Aaron."[25]

Moses and Aaron are the archetypal souls corresponding to the *sefirot* of victory and acknowledgment respectively, the *sefirot* from which all levels of prophecy derive, according to Kabbalah. In Chanah's prayer, this Name of God is combined with the Name *Havayah* and corresponds in particular to the *sefirah* of victory/eternity.

In Kabbalah, the prophet Samuel personifies the ultimate rectification of the *sefirah* of victory/eternity, which had been blemished from the time that Esau's angel injured Jacob's thigh.[26] After Israel's victory over the nation of Amalek (Esau's grandson, and the arch-enemy of Israel and the Almighty), Samuel said: "the Eternity of Israel shall neither deceive nor regret, for no mortal is He to regret."[27] In this verse, Samuel calls God "the Eternity of Israel," "*Netzach Yisrael*," clearly associating his figure with this Name and the *sefirah* of victory/eternity.

שַׁדַּי · pronounced *Shakai*

This is the holy Name whose literal meaning is "the Almighty." In Kabbalah, it is generally associated with the *sefirah* of foundation, which like its name, refers to the base upon which all existence stands.

The sages reveal that God used the Name *Shakai* to halt the expansion of creation. The letters of this Name are thus seen as an acronym for the words "Who said 'enough' to His world,"[28] a description of the Creator. The Name *Shakai* represents God's power to limit creation's natural tendency to expand infinitely. More generally, limiting the natural tendencies of creation can be understood as performing miracles. Unlike the essential four-letter Name of God, *Havayah*, which is often associated with miracles that openly defy nature and its laws, *Shakai* is associated with those miracles that change the course of nature while remaining concealed and enclothed within these same laws. The power to limit the inertia of endless expanse is the classic example of such a concealed miracle.

The Name *Shakai* often appears together with the Name *Kail* as *Kail Shakai*. Before unleashing the ten plagues on Egypt, a series of supernatural miracles reflecting the power of *Havayah*, God compared the Name *Havayah*, now to be revealed to Moses and the Children of Israel, to the Name *Kail Shakai*, the Name by which He had revealed Himself to the patriarchs:[29]

> "And I appeared to Abraham, to Isaac, and to Jacob by *Kail Shakai*; but by My Name *Havayah* I was not known to them."

אֲדֹנָי ⋅ pronounced *Adni*

The Name *Adni*, literally means "my Master." In Kabbalah, it is associated with the *sefirah* of kingdom.

The Name *Adni* acts as a garb, a revelatory vessel, for the essential Name *Havayah*. The relationship between these two Names of God was first alluded to in God's words to Moses at the Burning Bush: "This is My Name forever and this is My Remembrance from generation to generation."[30] "My Name" refers to the Name *Havayah*, while "My Remembrance" (which can also be read as "My Enunciation") refers to the Name *Adni*. From this we learn that we are to pronounce the Name *Havayah* as *Adni* in prayer or when reciting a verse of the Torah.

The Name *Adni* (representing God's imminence) serves to reflect the Name *Havayah* (representing God's transcendence) as it manifests itself in the created dimensions of time and space.

🕸

To summarize this chapter, let us present the sanctified Names of God and their correspondence to the vessels of the *sefirot* in chart form:

crown כֶּתֶר
אֶהְיֶה

understanding בִּינָה
יְהוָה

wisdom חָכְמָה
יָה

knowledge דַּעַת
אהוה

might גְּבוּרָה
אֱלֹהִים

loving-kindness חֶסֶד
אֵל

beauty תִּפְאֶרֶת
יְהוָה

acknowledgment הוֹד
אֱלֹהִים צְבָאוֹת

victory נֶצַח
יְהוָה צְבָאוֹת

foundation יְסוֹד
שַׁדַּי

kingdom מַלְכוּת
אֲדֹנָי

Notes:

1. *Shulchan Aruch, Yoreh De'ah* 276:8.

2. Exodus 3:13-14.

3. Ibid. 15:2, 17:16.

4. See *Torah Or, Esther* 95a-d.

5. As alluded to in the verse, "Those things that are concealed are to God our God, and those things that are revealed are to us and our children" (Deuteronomy 29:28).

6. See the article "*Chedvah*: The Secret of Breathing," in the Hebrew volume, *Esa Einai*.

7. See p. 50 and p. 90.

8. This particular revelation of the Almighty was frequently discussed by the Ba'al Shem Tov using its Kabbalistic name: "the light that carries the burden of all worlds." (אוֹר הַסּוֹבֵל כָּל עַלְמִין).

9. Like letters, vowel signs have numerical values. Vowel signs are made up of lines and points. A point (which resembles a letter *yud*) equals 10, while a line (which resembles the letter *vav*) equals 6. Thus, the 7 points of the vowel signs under this Name total 70.

By making the letters readable, the Hebrew vowel signs "give life" to the letters and therefore in Kabbalah are considered to be the lights within the vessels (of the letters).

10. Genesis 1:3.

11. *Chagigah* 12a.

12. Genesis 1:1.

13. Not to be confused with the Hebrew word *ahavah* (אַהֲבָה), which means "love."

14. In fact, there is an entire volume of Chassidic teachings titled *Or Haganuz* written by Rabbi Yehudah Leib of Anipolya, a contemporary and close friend of Rabbi Shneur Zalman of Liadi, which interprets the significance of each of the implicit appearances of this Name in the Five Books of Moses.

15. Isaiah 41:7.

16. Ibid. 49:6.

17. Psalms 52:3.

18. Ibid. 89:3. There is another related Name, אֱלוֹהַ, pronounced *Elokah*, which generally signifies the Divinity inherent in the *sefirah* of loving-kindness. The two letters of *Keil* are also the first two letters of this Name.

19. Genesis 6:2.

20. See Exodus 22:8, and elsewhere.

21. There is another manifestation of the Name *Elokim* in the *sefirah* of acknowledgment. When in acknowledgment, *Elokim* appears in conjunction with the Name *Tzevakot* (אֱלֹהִים צְבָאוֹת), which we will discuss presently (see for example Psalms 59:6, and elsewhere).

22. Together, understanding, might, and kingdom represent the three periods or states of the feminine life-cycle. Kingdom represents the stage of being a daughter. Might represents the stage of being a sister. And, understanding represents motherhood.

23. In addition, when appearing in conjunction with the sanctified Name *Tzevakot* (יְהֹוָה צְבָאוֹת), this Name becomes the vessel of the *sefirah* of victory, as will presently be explained.

24. I Samuel 1:11.

25. *Berachot* 31b. *Ta'anit* 5b.

26. Genesis 32:23-33. As explained in chapter 6, victory corresponds to the right foot.
27. I Samuel 15:29.
28. *Chagigah* 12a.
29. Exodus 6:3.
30. Ibid. 3:15.

Connotations 10

In the Torah, God is referred to by many connotations or *kinuyim*, in Hebrew. While describing the Almighty, words that connote Him are not considered sacred Names that may not be erased. In addition to the Almighty's connotative descriptions in the Bible, there are others that have been passed down to us by the sages.

Biblical connotations describe the more anthropomorphic nature of the Almighty, such as that He is merciful, forgiving, etc. Kabbalah explains that each of the many connotations of the Almighty corresponds to a particular *sefirah*.

The Thirteen Principles of Divine Mercy

Of all the connotations of God found in the Bible, the most important are the Thirteen Principles of Mercy:[1]

> *Havayah; Havayah*: God, merciful, and gracious; of a patient countenance, and of great loving-kindness, and truth; who keeps acts of loving-kindness for thousands of generations; who bears iniquity, and transgression, and sin, and absolves…

In Hebrew, these principles are called *midot*, or attributes. The word *midot* permutes to spell *d'mut*, which means "likeness" (as in the verse, "Let us make man in our image after our likeness"). The Torah commands us to "be like God,"[2] that is to integrate His attributes into our lives and act as accordingly. The specific examples brought by the sages are the attributes of mercy and forgiveness: "Abba Sha'ul says: Be like Him; just as He is merciful and forgiving, you should be merciful and forgiving...."[3] Thus, God's connotations reveal those aspects of His character, which are best suited for refining our own character.

Of the Thirteen Principles of Mercy, God is most often referred to by the fourth, "the Merciful One." In the Talmudic literature, the Aramaic form of this connotation, *Rachmana*, is used almost exclusively in reference to the Almighty.

Another of God's attributes that is often used to refer to Him is *Elyon* (literally meaning, "the Supreme One," which in Yiddish is translated as the *Aibishter*).

The Thirteen Principles and the *Sefirot*

As mentioned earlier, though we normally speak of ten *sefirot*, in practice, when including the *sefirah* of knowledge, there are altogether 13, as the supernal crown divides into three heads. Clearly then the Thirteen Principles may be seen to correspond to the 13 *sefirot*.[4] Like in many other cases, taking the elements of both the principles and the *sefirot* in order draws the simplest and most straightforward correspondence. Thus, the first measure corresponds to the first head of the crown, the second to the second head, and so on. Let us first chart the correspondence between the Thirteen Princples and the *sefirot*:

unknowable head רָדְל״א
Havayah יְהֹוָה

head of nothingness רֵישָׁא דְּאַיִן
Havayah יְהֹוָה

extended head רֵישָׁא דַּאֲרִיךְ
God אֵ־ל

understanding בִּינָה
gracious וְחַנּוּן

wisdom חָכְמָה
merciful רַחוּם

knowledge דַּעַת
a patient countenance אֶרֶךְ אַפַּיִם

might גְּבוּרָה
truth וֶאֱמֶת

loving-kindness חֶסֶד
great loving-kindness וְרַב חֶסֶד

beauty תִּפְאֶרֶת
keeps acts of loving-kindness for thousands of generations
נֹצֵר חֶסֶד לָאֲלָפִים

acknowledgment הוֹד
[bears] transgression וָפֶשַׁע

victory נֶצַח
bears iniquity נֹשֵׂא עָוֹן

foundation יְסוֹד
[bears] sin וְחַטָּאָה

kingdom מַלְכוּת
absolves וְנַקֵּה

Beginning with the three heads of the crown, whose experiential manifestations are faith, pleasure, and will respectively, we wish to explain this correspondence. The Name *Havayah*, the essential Name of God, connotes here the two higher manifestations of the *sefirah* of crown. To understand this we must first note that traditionally, in the *Zohar* and the writings of the Arizal, crown is divided into two *partzufim* called *Atik Yomin* and *Arich Anpin*. However, the Arizal teaches, based on the *Zohar*, that the inner *partzuf*, *Atik Yomin*, actually divides into two heads, while the external *partzuf*, *Arich Anpin*, is a head unto itself. Thus, the two higher heads are connoted by the same Name, *Havayah*. The first *Havayah* connotes the transcendent and unknowable head of the crown that is experienced as faith in the soul. The second *Havayah* connotes the second head called "nothingness" because it is the source of all that was created, *ex nihilo*.

We saw above that the seemingly redundant appearance of the essential Name *Havayah* at the beginning of the Thirteen Principles of Mercy refers to two ways in which the Name describes the Almighty. One way refers to His essence as it transcends creation. The other way refers to God's essence as it manifests in creation. The unknowable head of the crown transcends creation altogether. The head of nothingness manifests as the ultimate life source within creation.

The lowest of the three heads, the extended head, corresponds to the Name אֵל, here translated as "God." In the previous chapter we saw that this is also the Name of God that corresponds to the vessel of loving-kindness. The adjective "extended," *arich*, is closely associated, even in English, with loving-kindness, as in the idiom "to extend kindness." As a root in Hebrew, this Name implies power. Indeed, the true signature of a powerful person is his ability to extend kindness infinitely. Not being able to do so demonstrates restrictions and an inability to act without limits.

"Merciful" refers to wisdom, and "gracious" (in the sense of "forgiving") to understanding. Like these two *sefirot*, "that never part,"[5] the idiom "merciful and forgiving" appears together many times in the Bible. As explained by the Torah commentaries,[6] mercy is aroused when *seeing* someone in distress, while forgiveness is aroused when *hearing* someone calling out in distress.[7] In Kabbalah, sight is associated with wisdom and hearing with understanding.[8]

The connotation "a patient countenance" (which in the *Zohar* and the writings of the Arizal is understood to include two Divine principles of mercy[9]) alludes to the two aspects of the *sefirah* of knowledge. Within knowledge (the source of the emotions of the heart), they are the source of loving-kindness and the source of might (the two primary emotions), identifying them with the right and left side, respectively, of knowledge. As we have seen above, the *sefirah* of knowledge lies directly under the *sefirah* of crown along the middle axis of the *sefirot*, and in our context reflects the crown's external *partzuf*, *Arich Anpin*. This is evident because the Hebrew "a patient countenance," *erech apayim*, is rendered in Aramaic as *Arich Anpin*. The Arizal teaches that the male and female components of the *partzuf Arich Anpin* are situated to its right and left respectively. These are the origins of the right and left sides of the *sefirah* of knowledge.

Chassidic teachings explain that phenomena associated with the right relate to reality uniformly and transcend individual shortcomings, while phenomena associated with the left are sensitive to faults and shortcoming. In the case of the two aspects of knowledge, or consciousness, the right side, exhibits patience by transcending the problems and arguments that abound in reality. An individual can be patient with misdeeds and improprieties by transcending them and focusing his consciousness on the goodness of the Almighty who guides the world to its ultimate good. The word for "patient," *erech*, is the Hebrew root of the Aramaic *arich*, which we saw above to mean "long," or "extended." This is the quality of loving-kindness, as noted.

The left side, on the contrary, must face the negative aspects of life head-on and is therefore forced to react by assuming many different stances, or countenances, depending on the situation at hand. The connotation "countenance" in the Thirteen Principles of Mercy is actually written in the Hebrew plural form, alluding to how at its lowest level of descent and contraction, the left side can no longer see the inherent unity that subsists throughout reality and experiences reality as a plurality. The word *apayim*, translated here as "countenance," is the plural form of the word *af*, which means "anger" (or "nose," the central feature of the face or countenance[10]), alluding to the harshness with which the left-side meets reality. Ultimately though, it is the right side that envelopes the left and provides it with an overriding context of goodness and unity.[11]

The connotation "of great kindness," is of course directly related to the *sefirah* of loving-kindness and does not require further explanation.

As explained above, the word "truth" possesses distinct meanings in Kabbalah and Chassidut. Truth as fulfillment is associated with the *sefirah* of foundation. Here, truth is associated with the *sefirah* of might, which in Kabbalah is identified with the attribute of Divine judgment.[12] Truth as a connotation implies God's judgment,[13] which is aimed at ensuring that each person receives that which he or she deserves.[14]

The next connotation, "who keeps acts of loving-kindness for thousands of generations" refers to the *sefirah* of beauty. Beauty, situated along the middle axis of the *sefirot* under knowledge, mediates between loving-kindness and might by including the essence of both (and so, in the *Zohar* and the writings of the Arizal, "who keeps acts of loving-kindness for thousands of generations" is understood to include two Divine principles of mercy, as above, in the *sefirah* of knowledge, with regard to the division of "a patient countenance" into two components). Like physical beauty, spiritual beauty is the product of the tasteful inclusion of many different elements together. The beauty of a family, or group of people, becomes most apparent when it is surveyed over many (thousands of) generations. "Who keeps acts of loving-kindness" refers to the right side of the *sefirah* of beauty, the side of loving-kindness. "For thousands of generations" refers to the left side of the *sefirah* of beauty, the side of might, for only by Divine might do our acts of loving-kindness remain intact for thousands of generations.

The next three connotations appear together in a single phrase describing God as He who "bears iniquity, transgression, and sin." God is always ready to forgive our sins, our misdeeds in action. The three *sefirot* that correspond to our powers of action are the triplet of victory, acknowledgment, and foundation. To understand in greater depth how these three principles of Divine mercy correspond to the *sefirot* of victory, acknowledgment, and foundation in particular, we need to note that according to Kabbalah these *sefirot* are the practical manifestation of the three *sefirot* of the intellect: wisdom, understanding, and knowledge. Thus, the three types of negative actions—iniquity, transgression, and sin—reflect the intellectual *sefirot*, in order.

The word for iniquity appears in the verse: "Happy is the man for whom God does not count his iniquity."[15] The Ba'al Shem Tov explained that this verse can also be read as: "Happy is the man, for whom not thinking about God, is iniquity." As explained in Chassidut, the essence of life is one's connection with the Almighty. Thus, the individual who considers an iniquity even a temporary lack of awareness of the Divine Presence is to be commended. As explained elsewhere, awareness of God depends on selflessness, the inner experience of wisdom.[16] In fact, in Hebrew, the letters of the word for "inquity" (עָוֹן), permute to form the adjective meaning "humble" (עָנָו), which is the revealed aspect of selflessness. Wisdom is manifest pragmatically as victory.

The legal meaning of "transgression" (פֶּשַׁע) in the Torah is related to the role of a guard. If the guard fails to watch his charge in an appropriate manner, then he is considered to have transgressed.[17] Such failure is inevitably the result of decreased levels of joy and energy, the inner experience of the *sefirah* of understanding, whose practical manifestation is acknowledgment.

The word for "sin" (חֵטְא) in Hebrew can more accurately be translated as error. Clearly, making a mistake is the product of not paying attention, not being conscious of the matter at hand. Sin/error thus corresponds in the mind to a disfunction of the *sefirah* of knowledge. In Chassidut, knowledge is defined as the ability to connect to other things. When knowledge does not function correctly it is hard to create any kind of relationship. When the disfunctional state of knowledge is manifest in practice it affects the *sefirah* of foundation, specifically in the form of what in rabbinic terminology is euphemistically called *sins of youth*—

unwarranted sexual behavior. In Kabbalah, foundation is identified with the procreative organ.

Finally, the last connotation, which we have translated as "absolves," literally means a state of immaculate spiritual cleanliness. "Absolves" is actually part of the three-word Hebrew phrase that means: "...and absolves and does not absolve." The sages interpret this as a conditional: God absolves the sins of those who repent but does not absolve the sins of those who do not. The conditional reflects a special quality of the sovereign whose judgment exercises the power of reward and punishment based on the conditional actions of the subjects.

Notes:

1. Exodus 34:6-7.
2. See p. 27, n. 2.
3. Jerusalem Talmud *Pei'ah* 1:1 (3a). When quoting this passage in the Talmud, Maimonides (*Hilchot De'ot* 1:6) lists eight more attributes/connotations of the Almighty that we are commanded to integrate into our lives; they are: holy, patient, great loving-kindness, righteousness, upright, sincere, brave, and strong. Following the lead of the correspondence of the Thirteen Attributes of Mercy to the *sefirot* to be described in the text (besides the most obvious correspondences, like "brave," *gibor*, to might, *gevurah*) these altogether 10 attributes enumerated by Maimonides can be corresponded to the *sefirot* in the following manner (note that "a patient countenance," literally, "slow to anger," a property most characteristic of a rectifed king, appears here as kingdom, whereas with regard to the Thirteen Principles it corresponds to knowledge; in Kabbalah it is explained that often kingdom reflects knowledge, in the secret of the mouth, kingdom, being situated between the head, the intellectual faculties, and the body, the emotive attributes):

crown כֶּתֶר
holy קָדוֹשׁ

understanding בִּינָה
forgiving וְחַנּוּן

wisdom חָכְמָה
merciful רַחוּם

might גְּבוּרָה
brave גִּבּוֹר

loving-kindness חֶסֶד
of great loving-kindness רַב חֶסֶד

beauty תִּפְאֶרֶת
upright יָשָׁר

acknowledgment הוֹד
sincere תָּמִים

victory נֶצַח
strong חָזָק

foundation יְסוֹד
righteous צַדִּיק

kingdom מַלְכוּת
a patient countenance אֶרֶךְ אַפַּיִם

4. See note 9.
5. *Zohar* III, 4a.
6. See Rabbi Abraham ibn Ezra on *ad. loc.*
7. This relationship is expressed in two verses in the prophets: "My eye will not have mercy…" (Ezekiel 5:11) and "He will indeed be gracious to you when he shall hear your cry…" (Isaiah 30:19).
8. See more in *The Art of Education*, pp. 106-9.
9. The Arizal, following the *Zohar*, starts the Thirteen Principles from the Name אֵל, which according to our account is the third. The two Names of *Havayah* are understood to be above the Thirteen Principles.

   The two "missing" principles are then introduced by splitting the two and three word attributes אֶרֶךְ אַפַּיִם and נֹצֵר חֶסֶד לָאֲלָפִים into four principles, which would then be: 1) patient, 2) countenance, 3) recalls acts of loving-kindness, 4) for a thousand generations. When drawing the correspondence between the Thirteen Principles and the *sefirot*, the Arizal and the *Zohar* begin from the lowest head of the crown, the extended head, with the two Names of *Havayah* implicitly corresponding to the two higher heads of the crown. The *sefirot* of knowledge and beauty are divided into two aspects each.

10. אֶרֶךְ אַפַּיִם literally means: long nose. The Ibn Ezra (on the verse in Exodus) explains that since anger is vented through one's nose, the longer a person's nose, the less prone he or she is to express their anger outwardly. Thus, the well known Jewish facial feature is an expression of God's infinite patience. In addition, the Ibn Ezra writes that one with a long nose is able to sweeten (i.e., rectify) one who has a short nose, and who therefore acts impulsively, as in the verse: "The short-nosed acts impulsively" (Proverbs 14:17), where "short-nosed" is translated as "quick-tempered."

11. More deeply, Chassidic teachings explain that the right side of knowledge is the precursor to the Divine soul, while the left side is the precursor to the animal soul. The initial role of the left side of knowledge is to deter the infant and child from those things that would cause harm. Because the left side descends deep into reality, it is prone to fall under the influence of the impure husks (*kelipot*), and thus hunger and the infant's subsequent cry for food, which saves it from starvation, eventually becomes a craving for food which is independent of hunger. Thus, it is the left side of knowledge that is sensitive to danger.

The right side, which develops later in life through the study of the Torah (which, in its entirety, is the Name of the One God), is faced with the task of re-uniting the left side with the person's original source in the Divine, and particularly in the Divine Will and purpose for his or her life.

12. As noted in "The Torah Academy," the academic discipline related to might is law—the study of judgment and the administration of justice.

13. See *Rosh Hashanah* 17b.

14. *Rashi*, Exodus 34:7.

15. Psalms 32:2.

16. See p. 104.

17. Exodus 22:8. *Baba Metzia* 36b, and elsewhere.

Words 11

IN THE INTRODUCTION TO PART III, WE NOTED THAT EVERY WORD IN the Torah in truth refers to God, the Creator of all. This is because nothing in our mundane reality has an existence independent of the Almighty. Without God's creative will bringing every object or interaction of our physical world into existence at every single moment, it would not be here. Thus, the words of the Torah, which literally refer to objects or interactions, also refer to the Divine attribute that enlivens them.

Just as *Havayah* refers to God's essence and connotations refer to His attributes, words in the Torah refer to His creative attributes and can also be seen to correspond to the *sefirot*.

Kabbalah defines the particular source of every word in the Torah using the terminology of the *sefirot*. Doing so provides insight into how each word can be treated as a universal symbol. Kabbalah employs a variety of techniques to determine the particular aspect of the Almighty that every word in the Torah refers to. By analyzing a word using Kabbalistic techniques, we are able to probe deeper and deeper into its meaning and to uncover its universal significance. Let us turn then to looking at how ten simple words that describe objects in the physical world correspond to the *sefirot*. The ten words are: darkness, lightning, thunder, water, fire, air, mountain, valley, rainbow, and stone. As is our custom, we will first arrange them according to the *sefirot*, and then explain each particular association in turn.

crown כֶּתֶר
darkness חֹשֶׁךְ

understanding בִּינָה
thunder רַעַם

wisdom חָכְמָה
lightning בָּרָק

might גְּבוּרָה
fire אֵשׁ

loving-kindness חֶסֶד
water מַיִם

beauty תִּפְאֶרֶת
air רוּחַ

acknowledgment הוֹד
valley בִּקְעָה

victory נֵצַח
mountain הַר

foundation יְסוֹד
rainbow קֶשֶׁת

kingdom מַלְכוּת
stone אֶבֶן

Meditating on this *partzuf* as a whole and visualizing its components helps formulate the relationship between them. One can imagine how out of the darkness of a stormy night a bolt of lightning suddenly illuminates the sky and is quickly followed by the loud clash of thunder. The lightning strikes the waters, energizing them like fire, as the wind blows above them. The wind continues onto dry land, forming its mountains and valleys. Finally, as the storm ends and day breaks, a rainbow is seen between the clouds, as all of nature passes over the earth symbolized by the stone.

The concealing nature of darkness is similar to the impalpable nature of God's essence that the *sefirah* of crown alludes to. One of the most beautiful Psalms describes how the Almighty "conceals Himself in darkness."[1] God's concealed nature is also the source of our unrevealed super-consciousness. Our inexpressable super-consciousness is revealed by the *sefirah* of wisdom, which like lightning, lights the darkness of the night sky. In Chassidut, the experience of wisdom is referred to as "a lightning bolt across the mind."

Like the *sefirot* of wisdom and understanding that are forever joined in unison, lightning and thunder come together. The sense of sight, which perceives lightning, corresponds to wisdom, while our sense of hearing, which perceives the thunder, corresponds specifically to understanding. Of thunder it is said, "The thunder of His might, who can understand?"[2] The sages teach us that God created thunder in order to "straighten the hearts of men."[3] A straight heart is a heart full of understanding, as in the words of the *Tikunei Zohar*, "understanding is the heart, and with it the heart understands."[4]

Most of us are probably familiar with the four elemental forms of matter of antiquity: water, fire, air, and earth. In Kabbalah, these four correspond to the *sefirot* of loving-kindness, might, beauty, and kingdom, respectively. We will return to how the earth is here represented by the stone.

The inner experience of the *sefirah* of loving-kindness, love, is likened to water, whereas the inner experience of the *sefirah* of might, fear or awe, is likened to fire. The prophet says that, "whoever is thirsty, go to water,"[5] with love, while fire causes one to flee, in fear. The blue of sea waters is the color of the *sefirah* of loving-kindness in Kabbalah, while the red of fire is the color of the *sefirah* of might.

In Hebrew, air or wind (רוּחַ) also means spirit. In the second verse of the Torah we read that, "the spirit [רוּחַ] of God hovered above the waters." When the two primary letters of "spirit" (the ר and the ח of רוּחַ) are placed before the three letters of the word "waters" (מַיִם), the result is "mercy" (רַחֲמִים), the inner experience of the *sefirah* of beauty. In other words, compassion is the spirit of life.

The mountains and valleys of the earth's topography complement one another, just as the two *sefirot*, victory and acknowledgment do. In *Sefer Yetzirah*, these two *sefirot* are described as the high and low extremes. As explained in chapter 7, these two *sefirot* also complement one another in our psyche. Victory is experienced as active trust in God, whereby one does all that is in one's power to be successful, assured that God has given him or her power to succeed. Acknowledgment is experienced as passive trust, whereby one acknowledges that everything is truly in the hands of Heaven and therefore one can only look up to the Almighty for one's success. The two states of trust, active and passive, are symbolized by the upward aspiring mountains and the lowly valleys of the earth. It is especially the mountains and valleys of the Land of Israel that reflect the two types of trust in the Almighty, as in the verse: "those who trust in God are like the mountain of Zion, which will never falter."[6] The first half of the verse describes the active trust that is likened to the mountain of Zion. The second half of the verse contains the word "falter," which in Hebrew also means fall, as in falling down into the valley. The valleys of the Holy Land thus represent the passive trust in God that no harm will be*fall* us.

The rainbow is the sign of God's covenant with humanity.[7] In Kabbalah, a covenant alludes to the *sefirah* of foundation. The most important covenant in the Torah is the one made between God and Abraham, the covenant of circumcision that Abraham and his descendants were commanded to perform in the male procreative organ. In the *Zohar*, guarding the covenant refers to an individual who is careful to never engage in any kind of forbidden sexual conduct. Such an individual is referred to as a *tzadik*, a righteous, holy person, of whom Scriptures say: "And the *tzadik* is the foundation of the world,"[8] for the *tzadik* upholds our covenant with the Almighty, ensuring the world's endurance and continual progress towards its ultimate goal, universal redemption.

In the *Tanya*,[9] Rabbi Shneur Zalman explains the Divine origin of the Hebrew word for "stone," אֶבֶן, in the Torah as follows:

> "Stone," for example, its (Hebrew) name *even* (אֶבֶן), indicates that its source is in the Divine Name, which numerically equals 52 (בֶן),[10] with a letter alef (א) added to it from another Name, for a reason known to the Creator. Now, the Name that equals 52 is itself of very supernal worlds, but through numerous and powerful contractions, degree by degree,

there descended from it a greatly diminished life force, until it could enclothe in the stone. And, this is the soul of the inanimate being, which gives it life and sustains it *ex nihilo* at every instant....

As mentioned above, the letter filling of the Name *Havayah* that equals 52 corresponds to the *sefirah* of kingdom. Additionally, the stone is made out of, and represents, the elemental earth, the lowest of the four elements of antiquity, which also corresponds to kingdom.

More than any other *sefirah*, kingdom symbolizes the piecemeal construction of a complex entity from simple building blocks. As explained in Kabbalah, kingdom begins from a singular point, which then undergoes a process of construction (from packets of energies that come from the *sefirah* of might). This process of building the kingdom is alluded to in the verse, "And [Jacob] took the stone and made it into a monument and said: 'Indeed, this is the house of God....'"[11] The stone turns into a monument which then becomes a house. In Kabbalah, this three-stage process is referred to as point-line-area,[12] or point-*sefirah-partzuf*.

Hearing God in Words

The Ba'al Shem Tov and the Chassidic masters that followed him revealed that not only is every written word in the Torah a holy Name of God but that if our hearts are attuned to God, indeed every word that we think, speak, or write (whether in Hebrew or in any other language) is a Divine Name. The great masters of Chassidut *understood* how each word that they heard or spoke referred to God, and actually created new Kabbalistic intentions (*kavanot*) even for the most secular terms in the local jargon.[13]

We are usually oblivious to the deep meaning in every human utterance. But indeed, we do not need to understand exactly *how* it is that a word refers to the Almighty. For a word we speak to be considered a Divine Name, it is enough that it be spoken out of the sincerity of one's heart in simple faith in the Almighty.

Thus, though it may seem that by emphasizing the simple service of the heart the Ba'al Shem Tov de-emphasized the Kabbalistic intentions on Divine Names, in fact, he expanded the domain of Divine Names to include all words spoken to God from the depth of the heart. Where the Arizal (and the Kabbalistic masters that followed him) stressed the importance of understanding and correctly utilizing the holy Names in the intentions of our prayers, the Ba'al Shem Tov stressed the importance of prayer as it comes from the heart. By doing so, the Ba'al Shem Tov also brought us closer to realizing the Talmudic sages' vision of "Would it be that a person would pray all day long."[14] By continually inundating our consciousness with awareness of God and of His omnipresence, indeed all of our spoken words become as prayers before the Almighty.

Any and every human utterance directed to God from the depth of one's heart is a prayer. For God, the utterance itself is equivalent to a Divine Name spoken with all of deepest possible intentions of Kabbalah. To illustrate this point we turn to one of the most famous stories of the Ba'al Shem Tov:[15]

> In the time of the Ba'al Shem Tov there was a certain Jewish community that had been spiritually incriminated and was facing its destruction. When the Ba'al Shem Tov saw the gravity of the situation he prayed profusely on Rosh Hashanah and Yom Kipur. During Ne'ilah, the concluding prayer of Yom Kipur, his students realized from his manner of prayer that the decree must be very harsh and they too invested all of their spiritual strength into their prayers and pleas that were accompanied by sobbing and tears that came from the depths of their hearts.
>
> When the rest of the congregation felt how strongly the Ba'al Shem Tov and his holy students were praying they also understood that the situation was grave and joined them in tears and prayer from the innermost points of their hearts. The din grew from moment to moment.

For some years a certain Jewish youth who worked as a shepherd would join the congregation in prayer on Rosh Hashanah and Yom Kipur. Being that he could not read or write, he would stand silently, never uttering a word, and stare at the chazan (cantor) and the people pray.

Being that he was a country boy he was familiar with and could mimick the different sounds made by animals like goats, sheep, and birds. Most important in his eyes was the sound made by the rooster. As he witnessed the commotion and emotional excitement of the congregation, as he heard the sounds of crying and weeping both in the men's and the women's sections, his heart broke inside his bosom and he cried out, in a great voice: "Kuku-Reka-Han, God, have mercy!"

When the call like the call of the rooster was heard in the synagogue everyone was struck with fear, but with the words "God, have mercy!" it became clear that it was the young shepherd.

Some of the congregants who stood near the boy scolded him in an effort to silence him and were even about to run him out of the building. But he told them: "I too am a Jew, and your God is my God as well." The old synagogue custodian, Joseph Yuzpa calmed everyone and told the shepherd to remain where he was.

A few moments after the incident with the shepherd the Ba'al Shem Tov's voice was heard and the voice of his students followed his as they finished the Amidah of Ne'ilah. The Ba'al Shem Tov's face shone with joy.

The Ba'al Shem Tov began repeating the Amidah with a special melody and recited the Shema, Baruch Shem, and Hashem hu Ha'Elokim with special energy. Then our teacher the Ba'al Shem Tov began to sing songs of joy.

When the Ba'al Shem Tov and his holy disciples sat down to the break-fast meal, he told them all that had happened.

When he endeavored to nullify the decree with his prayers, he himself was accused of encouraging Jews to live in agrarian towns and on crossroads where they might learn from the ways of their non-Jewish neighbors.

"When [in the heavens] they began to inquire as to the ways and state of those who lived in the country," he said, "I saw that the situation was critical... But, then suddenly, the sincere call of the young shepherd 'Kuku-Reka-Han; God have mercy' was heard. This sincere call caused a great deal of pleasure Above, and reached the highest levels and all the negative decrees were annulled from that community and from myself."

How was it that a simple peasant boy who could not read or write, could be the one responsible for God responding to the congregation's prayers by mimicking a rooster? The answer is that the boy cried from the depth of his heart. Why is it important for us to know that the sound that he made was the sound of a rooster? Because Chassidic teachings stress that when prayer is addressed with true feeling and originates in the heart even the call of the cock can be a holy Name of the Almighty.

As Kabbalah began to be revealed in the Middle Ages, many rabbinical sages were suspicious of its talk of the *sefirot*. They feared that people who would hear about Kabbalah and not study it sufficiently could be mistaken to think that when praying to God, one should address Him through the *sefirot* (something we addressed at the beginning of our discusssion of God's Names). In order to prevent this, one of the great Talmudic scholars[16] coined a phrase describing the proper intent that a person should have when praying: "I am praying to He whom the toddler addresses as God." Young children, in their simplicity and innocence, are untainted by the false notions and incorrect intellectual assumptions that plague the adult mind. A beautiful Chassidic story illustrates how a child intuits and addresses the essence of another:

Rabbi Shneur Zalman of Liadi, the Alter Rebbe wanted to "test" his young grandson, Menachem Mendel who would later become the third Rebbe of Chabad, the Tzemach Tzedek. He sat him on his lap and asked him: "Where is zaide [grandfather]?" The young Menachem Mendel pointed to his grandfather's head. The Alter Rebbe smiled and shook his head: "No. That is zaide's head. Where is zaide?" The child pointed to his grandfather's chest. Again the Rebbe smiled but shook his head: "No. That is zaide's heart. Where is zaide?" And so the exercise continued until the child stood in seeming bewilderment. He jumped off his grandfather's lap and went, so it seemed, to play outside.

Suddenly a sharp cry was heard from outside the Rebbe's window: "ZAIDE! ZAIDE!"

The Alter Rebbe rushed outside to see what had happened and was greeted with a grinning Menachem Mendel who chirped merrily: "Here is zaide!"

The young child realized that there was no "grandfather" that could be pointed at. Grandfather was the man who came running out to him when he called his name.

Similarly, God cannot be pointed at, for God is not corporeal. Nonetheless, there is nothing more real or more existing than God. So though God cannot be pointed at, He can definitely be beseeched and called, as long as the call originates from an innocent and pure intent to beseech the Almighty Himself, and not any of His external manifestations. In that sense, any call can be the Name of God. In fact, the more flimsy the relationship that the call has to Names that describe God's attributes or manifestations the more possibility that it has of breaking through mistaken intellectual barriers that continually distance us from the Almighty. So though the study of God's Names is not discouraged, one is encouraged to learn enough about them so that they do not become an additional barrier to opening an honest channel of heartfelt communication with the Almighty.

One of the most fundamental teachings of the Ba'al Shem Tov is that maturity (*gadlut*) must follow immaturity (*katnut*). Immaturity here refers to the innocent call of the child, by what ever word or name he chooses. Maturity means that one has studied and knows how to intend to God's Names in prayer according to the teachings of Kabbalah. God wants us to mature, just like a parent wants his child to mature. But there is something about youthfulness that we should never lose. Chassidim say, "A Chassid is always young." And so in the words of the prophet, "For Israel is a youth, and I love him."[17]

The Four Categories of God's Names

As mentioned in the introduction to part III, the four categories of God's Names that we have discussed in the last four chapters correspond to the four letters of God's essential Name, *Havayah*, in the following manner:

קוצו של י (tip of *yud*)	crown	the ineffable essence of the Almighty
י (*yud*)	wisdom	essential Name, *Havayah*
ה (*hei*)	understanding	sanctified Names
ו (*vav*)	loving-kindness thru foundation	connotations and Kabbalistic Names
ה (*hei*)	kingdom	all words in the Torah and words spoken with awareness of God

Let us explain this correspondence. As stated earlier, all Names of God illuminate a certain quality or aspect of the Divine. However, the objective essence and nature of the Almighty is ineffable; human thought and human speech cannot fathom or capture any of it. Therefore, the essence of the Almighty is merely hinted at in the dimensionless tip of the letter *yud*.

The essential Name of the Almighty, *Havayah*, is the closest possible human connotation of the Almighty's essence. It is God's proper Name, which can only be pronounced as written in the

Temple, when in a state of complete and total nullification before Him, the inner experience of the *sefirah* of wisdom. When hearing the High Priest pronounce God's essential Name on *Yom Kipur*, the holiest day of the year, the people would fall and level to the ground, also in utter self-nullification before the Almighty.

The sanctified Names of God in the second category serve as the vessels into which the essential Name (with its variant meditational vocalizations) enters, just as the soul enters the body. The first *hei* of the Tetragrammaton is likened to a vessel, body, or hall (*heichal*), which the letter *yud* enters and inseminates with holiness.

Havayah and the sanctified Names illustrate the manner in which the two letters *yud* and *hei* of the Tetragrammaton are inseparable, for the Names in both categories may not be erased and form a distinct legal category in various facets of Jewish law.

The third category of connotations corresponds to the letter *vav* of the Tetragrammaton, or the six *sefirot* from loving-kindness to foundation, which in Kabbalah are called *midot*, or measures. The word *midot*, measures, is specifically related to the letter *vav* of the Tetragrammaton whose numerical value, six, alludes to the six spatial directions (up, down, front, back, left, and right).[18]

Finally, the manner in which all the words of the Torah, and even more so, all human utterances spoken with an awareness of the Almighty, comprise the fourth category of Names corresponds to the final letter *hei* of the Tetragrammaton. The last *hei* also corresponds to the world of Action, the lowest of the worlds described in Kabbalah.[19] In Kabbalah, the World of Action is considered relatively more disconnected from God than the other worlds, and is normally void of His revealed Presence. In the verse describing the four worlds, Emanation, Creation, Formation, and Action, the world of Action is connected to the three higher worlds by the word "even": "All that is called by My Name and in My honor, I created, I formed, I even (*af*) acted [i.e., made]."[20] Bridging the World of Action with the three higher worlds and bringing awareness of God to it requires special attention, to which the word "even" alludes.

The Ba'al Shem Tov was often heard saying the word *af*. When Rabbi Shneur Zalman was brought to trial in 1797 in Czarist Russia on charges that he and the Chassidic movement were seditious this fact was brought as evidence by the prosecution. They claimed that *af* meant anger in Hebrew and that the Ba'al Shem Tov had been trying to aggravate God and make Him angry with the non-Jews. The Alter Rebbe did not reveal to the judges the Ba'al Shem Tov's true intention, but according to one Chassidic interpretation, by saying *af*, the Ba'al Shem Tov was referring to the word "even" in the above verse. He was bridging the spiritual rift between the world of Action and the higher worlds. By constantly repeating this word, the Ba'al Shem Tov was bringing God's healing Presence and goodness more and more into our plane of reality. He was making it possible that every spoken word be a Name of God.

Now that we have examined the four levels of the Names of the Almighty, we may note that over the generations, Kabbalah has revealed a plethora of holy Names derived in various manners from the Biblical text. Such are the 72 three-letter Names of the Almighty, the Name of 42 letters, the Name of 22 letters, and the like. The study of these Names is left for a more advanced text. But the more advanced text will also end with the need for a more advanced text, and so on forever.

And so we conclude with the essence of the wisdom of Kabbalah, "The ultimate knowledge is to know that we cannot know."[21] There is always more to know and all of our knowledge is less than a drop in the ocean.[22] Only the one who strives to know more and more, truly comes to know that we can never know God, for He is infinite and we and our minds are finite. At the end, we stand before Him in perfect awe.[23]

Notes:

1. Psalms 18:12.
2. Job 26:14.

3. *Berachot* 59a.

4. Introduction to *Tikunei Zohar*.

5. Isaiah 55:1.

6. Psalms 125:1.

7. Genesis 9:13.

8. Proverbs 10:25.

9. *Sha'ar Hayichud Veha'emunah*, ch. 7.

10. See p. 143.

11. Genesis 28:17.

12. *Eitz Chayim, Sha'ar* 30, chapter 7. See Rabbi Dov Ber Schneersohn, *Torat Chayim* 65d, notes 52 and 53.

13. Famous among these in our generation was the Kabbalistic interpretation of the English word "now," by the Lubavitcher Rebbe. The Rebbe explained that "now" written in Hebrew, נאו, equals 57, the value of the union of two of God's Names, *Kail* (31) and *Havayah* (26). These two Names appear together in a verse in Psalms (118:27), "*Kail Havayah* shall enlighten us." As we have seen, *Kail* is the name of love and *Havayah* is the Name of compassion. The Rebbe taught that together, Divine love and compassion are the source of enlightenment and immediate salvation—now!

14. *Berachot* 21a.

15. Rabbi Yosef Yitzchak Schneersohn, *Kuntras Torat Hachassidut*, p. 6-7.

16. *Shut Harivash*, 157.

17. Hosea 11:1. In the *Tanya* (end of chapter 37), the Alter Rebbe explains that when learning Torah a person should feel like a young child calling out to his father to be with him. This feeling causes the Divine Presence to indeed rest upon that person while studying the Torah.

18. See more in *Living in Divine Space*.

19. See chapter 8.

20. Isaiah 43:7.

21. *Bechinat Olam* 13, 45. *Ikarim* II:30. *Shnei Luchot Habrit* 191a (37c). See especially *Keter Shem Tov*, 3.

22. See Rabbi Shneur Zalman's *Likutei Torah, Shir Hashirim* 9b.

23. In the words of Moses: "*Havayah* commanded us to observe all these statutes, to fear *Havayah* our God for our eternal good, to give us life as on this day" (Deuteronomy 6:24).

Subject Index

Bibliographic Index

Proper Names Index

Gematria Index